THE HEALING YOGA MANUAL

SWAMI AMBIKANANDA SARASWATI

PHOTOGRAPHY BY LAURA KNOX

THE HEALING YOGA MANUAL

WORK WITH YOUR
CHAKRA ENERGY CENTRES
TO INCREASE YOUR VITALITY

Eddison Books Ltd

This edition published in Great Britain in 2019 by
Eddison Books Limited
www.eddisonbooks.com

British Library Cataloguing-in-Publication data available on request.

ISBN 978-1-85906-429-0

10 9 8 7 6 5 4 3 2 1

Printed in China

PLEASE NOTE

The author and publisher cannot accept any responsibility for misadventure or injury resulting from the practice or application of any of the principles and techniques set out in this book. Not all exercise is suitable for everyone. It is recommended that you consult your doctor or healthcare professional before embarking on this or any other exercise programme. Do not force or strain your body to achieve any of the postures. This book is not intended as a substitute for medical attention, diagnosis or treatment; if you are in any doubt about any aspect of your condition, please refer to a medical professional.

CONTENTS

DEDICATED TO MY GURU,
SWAMI VENKATESANANDA SARASWATI

'Yoga is all those practices that enable us to discover health – which is not an absence of the symptoms of illness – but which is wholeness and holiness, an inner state of being in which there is no division at all.'

PREFACE

Yoga is now ubiquitous. You can find classes across the globe in workplaces and schools, health centres and studios, prisons and spas. It is estimated that, in the UK alone, yoga generates over £800 million in revenue a year. Yet, just over 120 years ago, yoga had hardly left the shores of India, where it originated as a particular philosophy within Hinduism.

In 1893, a fiery, saffron-clad monk stepped onto a stage in Chicago at the Parliament of World Religions and began a brief address with the words 'Brothers and sisters of America ...' With this, Swami Vivekananda brought the entire audience to their feet, in a two-minute standing ovation. 'Yoga' – a word that comes from Sanskrit, the mother of all Indo-European languages – means 'to join'; it also means 'togetherness' – and the Swami had reminded the audience of our togetherness, which transcends all divides. Yoga as a world phenomenon had arrived.

In the West, the search for the eternal has been largely abandoned and we have lessened our reach, aiming instead for health and longevity. Yoga, with its array of movements, seems to promise that. However, that is not all yoga offers. Yoga is a vast philosophy and practice that meets us on our mats in a gym, where we strive for a healthy body, but also guides us in a spiritual search for knowledge of ourselves.

The great Bengali poet Rabindranath Tagore lamented, 'When will I find myself complete in myself?' In our consumerist societies this has become the cry of many. The next 'thing' or 'experience' that we buy does not satisfy for long. It is here that yoga reveals a treasure: a map for journeying to a self that transcends body and mind. It is a difficult journey, as it requires encountering ourselves, and there is no way around this but through it. This book presents the panchatattva, or five great elements – part of yoga's map which provides an understanding and acceptance of ourselves as we are now, while simultaneously showing us how we can navigate the journey deeper within, where true healing awaits.

Swami Ambikananda Saraswati

INTRODUCTION TO YOGA

... think of it like this –
Imagine that the true Self is seated in the back of a chariot.
The body is the chariot and awareness (buddhi) is the driver.
The reins that the driver is holding are the mind (manas).

The senses (indriyas) are the horses that those reins lead to,
And the world with its many objects is the terrain the chariot moves along.
The Self, when it is in harmony with the body, mind and senses,
Is the enjoyer of the world and the doer of all actions.
So say the wise.

THE KATHA UPANISHAD, CHAPTER 1, VERSE 3
translated by Swami Ambikananda Saraswati

PLEASE NOTE

The appropriate Sanskrit transliteration has been used where Sanskrit terms appear in headings. For ease of reference, however, please note that standard phonetic spellings have been used within the text.

When we make the space in our overcrowded schedules, and on the floors of our homes, to practise our yoga postures, what is it that we are hoping to accomplish? What magic do we expect of yoga that we cannot get elsewhere? Yes, yoga does have the power to release muscles from their habitual state of tension and return them to their resting length. And it can certainly increase the mobility of our joints, restricted by years of sitting and standing with little regard or respect for the body's form and structure. But will it bring good health? Will it make us live any longer?

My guru, Swami Venkatesananda, a world-renowned yogi, died at the age of sixty-two after suffering from heart disease for a number of years. Indeed, in the West we have seen yogis of all methods who have taught their message and then died after a more-or-less average lifespan. Does this mean the promise of yoga has failed? And if a longer life is not the promise, what is it that draws us to yoga and makes us dedicate precious hours of our lives to it?

Perhaps what calls us to yoga in this technological world of instant delivery and smart machines is that we are beginning to understand the vision of the rishis (seers) of India from many thousands of years ago. Maybe we had to come through the industrial and technological revolutions in order to begin to ask the right questions about our own existence in this time, to be able to understand the answers the rishis gave us from their time.

One of the most beautiful ancient Sanskrit texts associated with yoga is the dialogue between the goddess (Devi) Shakti and the god Shiva. The dialogue begins with the goddess posing Shiva a question:

The Devi asked,
'God, god – O Greatest of all the Gods –
Shower me with your grace
By giving me that knowledge
Through which I may attain perfection.'

Shiva replied,
'The tattva, oh Great Devi,
Are the cause of this Universe
And they will bring about
Its dissolution.
To achieve perfection
You must know the tattva.'

(SVARAYOGA, AN ANCIENT SANSKRIT TANTRIC TEXT)

Thus the promise of yoga is perfection, which embraces health, happiness and the quality of our lives, no matter how long we live. And, as we shall see, health isn't an absence of disease, and happiness isn't an absence of tragedy. Swami Venkatesananda, along with the many yogis who brought us this wisdom from the East, lived this perfection. Every day of his life was lived to the full, in a wholeness and with a dynamic quality that can only be called 'human perfection'. In the pages that follow, we will explore how coming to 'know the tattva' – the 'vitalities' – through the philosophy and practice of yoga can move each and every one of us closer to discovering our own innate perfection.

ANCIENT WISDOM

It would seem that, no matter who we are or what the measure of our personal power and authority may be, we are called upon to live even while the purpose of life remains mysterious. We are here, alive – but few claim to know why. And not knowing this so bedevils us that we seek either answers or distractions. Yoga is a way of seeking answers to this mystery.

Three systems existed on ancient Indian soil: yoga, samkhya and tantra. They were neither science nor religion, yet each had elements of both. They come to us from an ancient human past, long before we began to see ourselves reflected in the machines we create, or divide ourselves into parts and fragments that can be used and replaced. These systems didn't deny the experience of a universe made up of 'parts', but they always pointed us to its wholeness. A life in which the disposable machine takes precedence over a 500-year-old tree or a fragile flower robs us of what these systems prized most highly: vitality. A machine doesn't possess vitality – rather, it has a measured amount of energy poured into it to get it to work. We humans use and transform the energy of the universe to create our own energy. The success with which we do this can be measured by the quality of our vitality, which we must use to discover and fulfil our purpose, or *dharma*.

To understand yoga, we must have some knowledge of Hinduism and yoga's sister sciences, samkhya and tantra. Their origins are buried in the depths of India's ancient past.

DISTANT ORIGINS

Around 10,000 BCE, human beings learned to grow crops, which had a profound impact on the social order and the environment. Thereafter, civilizations began to appear alongside great rivers – the Nile in Africa, the Euphrates in the Middle East and the Indus in India. The civilization of the Indus, which has become known in archaeology as the Harappa culture, produced at least two great cities – Harappa and Mohenjo Daro (although both appear to have even more ancient civilizations buried under them). Fragments of terracotta pottery unearthed at these sites show that yoga postures were already being practised at this time. Yoga continued to evolve throughout Indian history as both a philosophy and a set of practices assimilating aspects of the analysis of samkhya and the practical knowledge of tantra, while remaining an independent system.

Samkhya and tantra

Tantra was an empirical system of agricultural, medicinal, mathematical and other kinds of practical knowledge about the world. Samkhya, on the other hand, was founded by one of the most revered sages of India, Kapila. Its philosophy delved into the mystery of life by examining the different parts of a human being's experience in order to arrive at a complete knowledge of its wholeness. The word 'samkhya' means 'the count', and each of the parts samkhya enumerated was called a 'tattva'. The Sanskrit word 'tattva' literally means 'thatness'. It's also 'that' (tat) – the divine inherent in, and inseparable from, all things. The tattvas are the notes of the symphony in which the life of matter and the life of the spirit are woven together as one. The tattvas of samkhya, which the yogis adopted, can be said to be the active principles of the divine.

The tattvas begin with Purusha and Prakriti. Purusha can be translated as 'consciousness' and Prakriti, usually translated as 'creation', can just as appropriately be translated as 'evolution'. Prakriti is the material evolution of Purusha: they are inseparable, like milk and its whiteness, or sugar and its sweetness. From Prakriti all the other tattvas evolve, while Purusha remains the silent and uninvolved witness. See opposite for samkhya's enumeration of the tattvas, which here are given their original Sanskrit spellings.

From Prakriti, an intelligent awareness evolves called *buddhi* (sometimes called *mahat*, or The Great One). From this awareness arises the idea of 'I' – the *ahamkara*. This is the social person – the person we are brought up to believe we are. From these first tattvas evolves invisible matter in its most subtle form: the *tanmatra* – sound, touch, form, taste and smell. From the tanmatra emerge the *panchatattva* (also called *mahabhuta* or 'great elements') consisting of space, air, fire, water and earth, which in turn give rise to the five means of knowledge, the *jnanendriya*: hearing, touch, sight, taste and smell. These means of knowledge create five means of action, the *karmendriya*: speech, movement of the hands, walking or movement of the feet, procreation and excretion. From all of these means of knowledge and action evolves *manas*, the mind, which acts as a relay station between them.

Thus, to the ancient yogis a human being was much more than a 'thinking machine'. The philosophy and bodywork the yogis developed envision and celebrate the complexity of a human being, particularly the interaction and unity of the tattvas in human experience.

THE TATTVAS OF YOGA

These tattvas of yoga are all within the encompassing tattva of Ishvara. This is often incorrectly translated as 'Lord' or 'God', but literally means 'That which is'. As with many Sanskrit terms, there is no exact translation and it's better to use the Sanskrit term, then explore its meaning.

PURUṢA **PRAKṚTI**

1 BUDDHI – awareness or intelligence – is the highest form of Prakriti.

2 MANAS – mind – is that form of Prakriti that takes in information from the senses and creates our 'world'.

3 AHAṀKĀRA – the sense of an 'individual self' – evolves from the activity of Manas. Ahamkara literally means the 'I-maker'.

Together these form *chitta*. The sage Patanjali (see page 14) defines yoga as '*yogaś citta vṛitti nirodhaḥ*' – 'Yoga is the stilling of the movement of thought in chitta.'

This evolution of Prakriti continues into the remaining tattvas.

ĀKĀŚA TATTVA
Space, sound, speech, ear

VAYU TATTVA
Air/wind, touch, hands, skin

AGNI TATTVA
Fire, sight, feet, eyes

APAS TATTVA
Water, taste, reproductive, tongue

PṚTHVI TATTVA
Earth, smell, excretive, nose

The three gunas

Tied in with this metaphysics there are three essential properties of Prakriti: the three *gunas* – phases of vitality – known as *rajas*, *tamas* and *sattva*. All of the tattvas, apart from Purusha, are subject to these.

Everything in the world of matter is in a constant state of change, and this change was called rajas. But if there is rajas, then its opposite, inertia, is also present, and this was called tamas. Thus expansion and contraction, or transformation and conservation, exist side by side. A third quality, sattva, was then added. Unlike tamas, this third guna has no mass and, unlike rajas, no movement. If neither mass nor movement is active, then a state of sattvic harmony and equilibrium exists.

The three gunas, present everywhere and in everything, don't mix and blend but rather react with each other. Each seeks dominance over the others. In the darkness of night, day will begin its ascendancy, and vice versa. We sleep and we awaken to a renewed energy and activity. After a day's activity, we are overcome by sleep. Throughout our lives, everything we touch, eat or do is governed by these three influences – rajas, tamas and sattva, our constant companions.

The gunas permeate everything through the power of *prana*. Anyone who has ever attended a yoga class in the West will already be familiar with this word. It originates from the Sanskrit root verb *pri* which means 'to fill'. Prana is that power through which matter comes into being and organizes itself by means of the tattvas, under the direction of the gunas. Often translated as 'energy', prana is more correctly translated as 'vitality'. Energy is measurable, vitality is not – and yet we experience keenly its ebb and flow through us.

Modern medicine, as soon as it adopted a mechanistic approach to the body, lost contact with the concept of vitality. As a noted French psychiatrist, Jacques Lacan, pointed out in the 1960s, as soon as medicine began to look in the body for the machine, energy disappeared. In Lacan's view, Sigmund Freud was the first person to realize this. In an attempt to return energy to the body, Freud introduced the concept of 'libido' – an energy or drive that he 'organized' around our sexual functioning.

For the yogis, the concept of vitality never disappeared, and they organized it around the tattvas. This vitality, or prana, was at the disposal of everything that evolved from Prakriti: from the individual consciousness (buddhi) and the idea-of-I (ahamkara) to the panchatattva – earth, water, fire, air and space. When we are moving, thinking and grasping ideas quickly, then we can be said to be organizing our vitality under the auspices of air. When we are thinking clearly and systematically, we can be said to be organizing it under the auspices of space. When we become tactile and gregarious, joyous and generous, we can be said to be organizing our vitality under fire, and when we become withdrawn and thoughtful we are organizing it around water. Organizing vitality around earth makes us grounded and supportive. Thus to the yogi and the samkhya philosopher, we were never reflected in the machine, but rather in the vast and creative objects of nature.

Through this enumeration of creation, samkhya sought to penetrate beyond the veil of matter and the social personality to the mystery of life, to discover the happiness beyond our immediate situation. Yoga has given us the means to reach that goal, while tantra offers its vast stores of knowledge about how the world of creation works.

Reconciling our awareness

To the enumeration of the tattvas, the yogis added one more: a twenty-sixth tattva, Ishvara. 'Ishvara' literally means 'that which is'. This is the closest the yogis came to referring to what is often called God (which the Sanskrit texts known as the Vedas would later refer to as Brahman). To understand the full mystery of life and arrive at perfection (*sat*), full consciousness of who we are (*chit*) and happiness (*ananda*), which the yogis postulated are our birthright, we have to reconcile our individual awareness with Ishvara. There has to be a perfect alignment of one with the other. The great yoga sage Patanjali referred to this alignment in his *Yoga Sutras*, chapter 1, verse 23:

Ishvara pranidhanad va
Or [this state of yoga may be achieved]
by alignment [of the individual awareness]
to Ishvara.

So, for the ancient yogis, a necessary part of yoga practice was being present to the Presence that isn't immediately apparent to us.

THE MEANING OF YOGA

In its origin and at its core, the word 'yoga' implies movement. There are some 2,200 verbal 'roots' in Sanskrit, and these roots remain inactive until they're changed and charged to become active. Yoga comes from such a root form – *yuj*, 'join', which through its process of adaptation becomes an active verb, *yoga* – 'to join'. So the inherent perspective of yoga is that we are fragmented, and that a joining, or a making whole, is necessary. For joining to happen, various criteria are necessary – although movement is the first. To bring two or more things together, 'I' must move them from their present position of apparent separation and bring them into alignment.

Yoga is movement, but not all movement is yoga. Only movement that 'brings together' can be called yoga. The movement that brings the physical, intellectual, emotional and spiritual aspects of our being into alignment may be called yoga. The movement that brings the individual life into alignment with the greater continuum of life, or Ishvara, may be called yoga. And the ultimate movement that absorbs all the tattvas into buddhi and the buddhi into Ishvara, may be called yoga. It's this realization of our universal nature that is the goal of the movement of yoga.

MATTER, VIBRATION AND DUALITY

According to this ancient teaching, we appear as matter not because we've vacated our universal realm to live on earth, but because we've altered our 'vibration'. Through this alteration, we appear to exist in a confined space and time, but in reality we stretch forwards and backwards into infinity. This vibration is what the samkhyas and the yogis called the tattvas – the phases of evolution of Prakriti – and while these occur in infinity, they're localized in our bodies also.

The followers of Vedic philosophy questioned existence. Why are we here? What are we? Six great systems of philosophy would evolve from this questioning and would become known as the *darshanas*, or philosophies. Yoga was – and is – one of these. Some of these philosophies would see the world and matter as an illusion to be overcome, but for others, like yoga, creation is an expression of a Divine Presence called simply Ishvara (that which is; see 'Reconciling our awareness', opposite). For the yogi, our work is to connect with inner Presence, and the body was included in our search for it.

Yoga and the panchatattva

Five of the tattvas, known as either the panchatattva (*pancha* means 'five') or the mahabhutas ('the great elements'), offer us a unique way of using our yoga practice to return to a realization of the wholeness of our nature as the yogis perceived it. The panchatattva are earth, water, fire, air and space, and the tanmatras, jnanendriyas and karmendriyas (see page 12) can be said to vibrate and resonate from and within these five tattvas.

At the dawn of the nineteenth century, science took an exciting turn that mirrored the vision of the yogi. Physicists discovered that the atom – once understood to be the smallest unit of matter – was not solid at all. Inside the atom, they found that matter exists as both a wave and a particle. It follows, then, that material existence – us and all the solid things we can see, hear, smell, touch and taste – has a dual nature: it exists as both a solid particle defined in space and as a unlocalized wave. Furthermore, this 'wave state' contains all the probable locations that the particle state might occupy.

We are matter, and therefore this dual nature applies to us also: we are individuals occurring in a certain time and space, but we are also a dynamic and universal 'probability wave'. Perhaps it's this that the yogis were referring to when they spoke of prana, which, like the probability wave, contains and determines all the possibilities and potential of our physical existence.

Within this prana are the five 'patterns' – the panchatattva. As prana flows through us and takes on the vibrations of these panchatattva, we are formed in body, mind and awareness. This means that, while we are all the same and made of the same 'stuff', each of us is also a unique expression of prana. Our uniqueness is born of the activity, potency and organization of the panchatattva. For example, prana flowing through the earth (Prithvi Tattva) will give us qualities of stability and cohesion, while prana flowing through water (Apas Tattva) imparts fluidity of mind and body along with creativity. When this same prana flows through fire (Agni Tattva), it will give the capacity to transform information into ideas and food into nourishment. Yet when it flows through air (Vayu Tattva) it will give us movement and through space (Akasha Tattva), organization.

We each possess all these qualities imparted by the panchatattva. But in each of us they will form a unique hierarchical pattern. For example, if Prithvi Tattva (earth) predominates, it will impart negotiation skills and supportiveness – the nature of earth being to see both sides and lend support to all. If Vayu Tattva (air) predominates, though, it will give leadership skills and a mind like quicksilver.

This is the exploration of the Panchatattva Way of Yoga. It enables self-discovery as part of the journey towards discovering a greater 'self', in which we are not merely all equal, but one. This, to the yogi, is considered the ultimate purpose of all human existence, whatever else we are engaged in. Within this, they promise, lies full consciousness of our true and blissful nature.

When we organize our asana practice according to the panchatattva, we seek to find both their reflection in ourselves and the unchanging divinity within them.

SELF-DISCOVERY AND SELF-DISCLOSURE

The ancient yogis tell us we place far too much emphasis on the ahamkara, the idea-of-I. This social self is no more than the person we were brought up to believe we are. For example, I am a woman – that's a biological fact. However, what a woman is supposed to be is a cultural and social construction that changes from place to place. To discover what it truly means to be a woman, I have to work my way through these constructs. That's how it is with the ahamkara. The socially constructed 'I' is made up of others' judgements and values. Discovering the truth behind this shadow 'I' requires working through what is given to us as 'I'. Clinging to this ahamkara, which distinguishes and holds itself apart from the rest of creation, is the cause of our sorrow, say the yogis.

BEGINNING THE JOURNEY

I met Swami Venkatesananda when I was just twenty, and frightened and confused about my future. After hearing him speak, I decided to look into yoga as a possible way out of my confusion. I used to joke with friends and say things like, 'Ah well, I'll give this yoga five years and if it doesn't work it's back to sex, drugs and rock and roll'. Then, as is my nature, I threw myself into its practices. I sat for hours in meditation each morning, sweat pouring down within five minutes as I brought every ounce of effort I had to controlling a wild, untamed mind. I went to every hatha yoga class I could find, by just about every master, from India to America, and forced my body to yield to my will. Swamiji just watched for a couple of years – letting me go with the bit between my teeth. Then one day he said quietly, 'It won't work until you come to it empty-handed'.

I had no idea what he meant, and he had to help me come to an understanding that overcoming body and mind through will was not the practice of yoga. All ambition, all determination, all self-effort had to be dropped, and yoga had to be approached empty-handed. It had to be an engagement of the individual in self-exploration and self-discovery – not an exercise in power and control. This is only possible once the will 'to do' has somehow been loosened. I have come to call his method of practice the Panchatattva Way, in which I use the panchatattva as a model for self-discovery through the practices of yoga.

I had to begin by seeing myself reflected in nature – to know that I was made up of the same stuff as the vast expanse of space, the whistling wind, the blazing sun, the fathomless oceans and the supporting earth. Swamiji helped me to bring myself into sharp enough focus to see which one of the five tattvas predominated in me and what the tattvas' 'pattern' of activity was.

I had always wanted to be like my father. When he walked into a room all eyes would turn to him. People would gather around him, listen to him, be fascinated by him. The tattva most powerful in him was fire, and this is what 'fire' is like: it draws people closer to it, and it charms and captivates. Fire did not predominate in me. My own perfection doesn't lie in being my father but in discovering and being myself.

Of course, the tattva of fire exists within me as it does within all of us, and now I have learned how best to harness its power when I need it. But for each of us, the beginning of the journey of the Panchatattva Way is to discover our own pattern, to look at nature and see what is reflected most strongly in us. In this lies your uniqueness and the doorway to your yoga practice as you begin to live a life that supports the natural flow of prana within your whole body–mind complex. You discover what it is to be more fully yourself. Then, those changes that will lead to renewed health will come naturally and without effort.

HEALTH AND HAPPINESS

For yoga to enable our self-discovery, we need a mature understanding of what health and happiness are. Was Swamiji unhealthy when he was suffering from heart disease in the final two years of his life? No, he always remained the most healthy person I have ever known.

The word 'health' comes from an Old English word *hǣlth* meaning 'whole'. Swamiji always remained whole – entirely integrated with the oneness of creation. In this wholeness, each part of his being was compassionately aware of every other part, allowing him to work and maintain relationships with his friends and disciples in a way that would not usually be possible for people in his condition. His body, although ailing, remained the embodiment of consciousness – happiness and health radiated out to everyone who encountered him. He was not bound to habitual ways of acting or reacting. There were no familiar old patterns in his responses to the world and the people he encountered. Rather, he remained always spontaneous – action and reaction emerging from a state of deep awareness. To experience wholeness, it's this state of awareness that has to be experienced. In it we are no longer strangers to ourselves – moved by reactions we are often bewildered by. In this awareness lies the possibility of wholeness. This isn't suppression of our emotions, but a joyful experience of them as a part of the wholeness that is self – and an understanding of that which is 'not self' but rather the construct of another, and that can therefore be released from our lives.

That's what we are seeking and what will bring about a true healing in our lives: a sense of wholeness in which we are not mere cogs in a wheel, living without purpose or meaning, but whole beings – aware of ourselves as a part of creation that's naturally, unashamedly and compassionately aware of every other part of creation. We need to learn to live as nature does, knowing that our experiences and our practices are not isolated from creation but an integral part of it. When we come to that realization, our lives suddenly have meaning: we no longer work for ourselves alone, but arrive at a transcendent purpose. Then we don't live with the fear of a self being consumed by disease, old age and death because we are in touch with a 'self' that exists outside of these things.

MAPPING THE TATTVAS

To bring us to a fuller understanding of this state, the yogis gave us the teaching of the five tattvas. Because we cannot leap from the idea-of-I into cosmic oneness, the yogis gave us a 'map'. We appear in this world, they said, through five sacrificial fires. These fires are formed by the tattvas and represent the stages of our descent from universal being to individual being.

First on the map is space, Akasha Tattva, the initial vibration, the intention of creation – both universally and individually. We are 'intended' by the universe long before we appear in our mother's womb. Next comes air, the atmosphere and even the wind – all these fall under Vayu Tattva. This is the stirring into activity – the intention giving rise to movement. Then comes fire, Agni Tattva – the spark is lit by the wind, and as the fire burns it transforms intention and potential into form. Next comes water, Apas Tattva. The ancient texts say that the clouds formed by the smoke of the fire release rain, bringing the sacred and pregnant life-fluids into being. Finally there is earth, Prithvi Tattva. The body, fully formed, emerges into the world: it is.

Through the sacred ritual of this creative universe we come into being. And our coming into being isn't an isolated event but one in which the whole universe has participated. But our physical birth hides our reality. Through it we find ourselves on a merry-go-round of waking, dreaming and deep sleep in which all purpose seems lost. These are the three states that physicality confines us to – until we choose to turn our vision from the material expanse before us to that inner consciousness, that inner seeing that the yogis called Adhyatma.

The five sheaths

The five tattvas bring with them the five bodies or sheaths – *koshas* in Sanskrit – that cloak our eternal and infinite reality and can only be uncovered through the inner vision of Adhyatma yoga. Not perceptible to our ordinary vision, through our yoga practice we develop the inner vision that comprehends and 'sees' that we are much more than the boundary of our skin reveals.

First, there is the dark, semi-awake causal sheath called *anandamaya kosha*. This first 'cloak' carries with it the taste of bliss of the true self and imparts the desire to return to that self. Then the faculty of intelligence, *vijnanamaya kosha*, manifests out of anandamaya kosha. In this cloak, we carry our powers of intellect, discrimination and awareness – the tools we need to return to the bliss. From the intellect emerges the mind, *manomaya kosha*. This is the cloak of many colours that carries all our confusion. To the yogis we aren't born 'empty' but come with a history. We bring with us into each life a particular baggage (which the yogis called the *prarabdha karma*). It's this that will give us our personal genetic structure and our particular personality, which will see the world in its particular way, carried in the manomaya kosha. From manomaya kosha, *pranamaya kosha* – the vital body – emerges. The final sheath to emerge is *annamaya kosha*, the food sheath, the physical body – the other four bodies made manifest.

The prana flows through these koshas in rivers called *nadis* (often also referred to as meridians, particularly in Chinese medicine). There are said to be 72,000 of these unseen nadis flowing through the body, delivering the universal vitality to each and every cell. Of these, three are considered of utmost importance: *sushumna nadi* – the golden pathway – *ida nadi* and *pingala nadi*. Sushumna nadi corresponds to the very centre of the spine but begins in the perineum (root of the genitals) and continues up to the crown of the head. It's described as having the brightness of a thousand suns, while remaining cool as a moonlit night. The ida and pingala nadis also begin at the perineum: ida to the left and pingala to the right of sushumna. Ida and pingala wind around sushumna in a double helix and terminate at the left and right nostrils.

Chakras

The nadis themselves have points of influence in their flow called *chakra* (meaning 'spinning wheel'). It's here that prana is 'organized' in its flow through the body and mind. Again, there are thousands of chakras throughout the body, but seven of them are of major importance. All seven occur in sushumna nadi. Five of them are under the influence of the panchatattva and organize the prana in accordance with their respective tattva. We will find out more about this organization in Part 2 (see pages 32–5). For now, it's more helpful to think of these tattvas, housed within the five chakras, in general terms, as creating the person that you uniquely are in this universe as well as helping you to discover the gift that you have brought. In this gift lies the purpose you have to fulfil before returning and making your way back through these five fires to your universal home. Only then do you depart the merry-go-round and exist in *turiya* – the fourth state of consciousness.

Kundalini: the mysterious power within

As long as we live our lives without engaging in the process of self-discovery, we never awaken and realize our full potential. The yogis actually gave a form to this potential – they called it *kundalini*. It's depicted as a snake, coiled and slumbering at the base of sushumna nadi. As we begin to engage in the yogic disciplines and delve deeper and deeper into the inner terrain of our being, this slumbering energy is brought to wakefulness. The goal of every yogi is to awaken kundalini and initiate and maintain its upward flow towards *Sahasrara* – the thousand-petalled lotus at the crown of the head. There, the individual potential, fully awakened and conscious of itself, is united with the divine cosmic force. This, to the yogi, is the moment of complete enlightenment.

LOSING BALANCE

Out of our idea of separation our pain is born. We look at objects outside of ourselves, and because they are really a part of us we are drawn to them. In this process, a disturbance will arise and we will develop an aversion to the object. Then we are caught between both loving and hating the object simultaneously. This, the yogis called *raga* and *dvesha*: love and hatred. And it's this raga–dvesha conflict that creates the imbalance and pain that becomes *samskara*. Samskaras are the penetrating responses that we develop every time we react rather than create. When someone 'pushes our buttons' and we respond in old habitual ways, that is samskara. Swami Venkatesananda used to call them 'some scars'. These 'scars' are wounds that haven't been given the healing grace of awareness but are opened and reopened by our inability to learn enough about ourselves to allow them time to heal.

Through the power of raga and dvesha we are caught in the net of *maya*. Often translated as 'illusion', maya is a power of Prakriti that has a will of its own: to sustain us on the merry-go-round, to keep us thinking of ourselves as a duality or multiplicity of parts that are never whole and complete. It mesmerizes us with a world that we are both drawn to and repulsed by through raga–dvesha. This world of maya is known as *samsara*, from the Sanskrit root *sr* – 'to slip'. It's the world in which we slip and slide between like and dislike, love and hatred. I may love intensely the idea of my individuality (even while disliking parts of it based on others' judgements), and I may hate anything that threatens it. But, as long as I'm in the slipping and sliding world of samsara, I won't discern the true nature of 'I'.

Neither asanas (yoga postures), pranayama (prana-control exercises that usually involve breathing practices) nor meditative practices will remove us from this world of sorrow until we stop using them to protect and defend the indefensible: the ahamkara. For our yoga practices to make sense, we must remove the impulses, ambitions and cravings for fulfilment of the ahamkara, and embark on the journey that will reveal what lies behind it.

What we often discover is a broken and impeded flow of prana through the nadis. As we swing from love to hate, like to dislike, the mind generates a mythology, which it keeps running to support this swing. The yogis called this *vritti*. It's the background dialogue of the mind that upholds and supports the activity of the ahamkara – and it's painful. Loving and being drawn to are bound with pain

Never go into your asanas 'cold'. Always give your muscles a gentle warm-up using some of the techniques shown on these pages. If you are already accustomed to 'salute to the sun' (surya namaskar – see pages 117–21), do a few rounds of half of the sequence very gently and slowly, signalling to your muscles your intention to awaken and stretch them. Many of the yoga postures build strength as well as opening and stretching the muscles. The method of doing them is always exactly the same: slowly, with mindfulness and attention to your body.

Above all, you should enjoy the warm-up. It's a way of encountering your body before you go into the deeper stretches and strengthening postures of yoga. Rush nothing. Tune into the breath and remember that the most valuable part of your practice is going to be the stillpoint.

STRETCHING THE POSTURAL MUSCLES IN THE BUTTOCKS AND HIPS

Sometimes forward bends are inhibited by tightness in the postural muscles in the lower back and buttocks. Use this technique to help release these before trying the powerful forward bends of yoga.

1 Sit with your legs stretched out in front of you. Bend one leg and place the foot alongside the opposite buttock.

2 Now bend the other leg and lay it on top of the bent leg, with the foot alongside the opposite buttock. Rest your hands on your feet.

3 Take a deep breath in, lengthening through the front of your spine.

4 Now breathe out and pivot forward from your hips. Hold this stretch for a few seconds, enjoying the unusual stretch deep in your buttock, then release.

5 Repeat the whole sequence with your other leg on top.

HAMSTRING STRETCH

Many practitioners spend years trying to lengthen the stubborn hamstrings at the back of the legs. Try this exercise, and also try the 'Muscle energy technique' exercise on pages 28–9.

1 Lie on the floor and hug your knees into your chest to gently stretch the postural muscles of the buttocks and lower back.

2 Straighten one leg down onto the ground.

3 Place a strap around the instep of the foot of the other leg and raise the heel to the ceiling.

4 Allow the leg to relax in this lengthening for a few seconds, then slowly begin to draw the front of the thigh down towards the hip and extend the heel towards the ceiling, creating a powerful stretch up the back of the leg.

5 Hold in this position for a few seconds, maintaining your breathing, then release and hug the leg into the chest, again for a few seconds.

6 Repeat with the other leg.

STRETCHING THE SPINE

The back is taken into powerful forward and backward bends during yoga asanas, so it's important to warm it up with a few simple exercises before attempting the bends. Try the exercises shown below, and the ones on pages 26–7, for a good all-round stretch.

FRONT AND BACK OF SPINE STRETCH

This stretching exercise is particularly good for limbering up the spine in preparation for both forward and backward bends.

1 Go onto all fours, with the heels of your hands under your shoulders and your knees under your hips (not pressed together).

2 Breathe in, and as you breathe out draw your abdomen up towards the spine, tuck your tailbone under, arch your back up and drop your head.

3 Breathe in and return to a neutral position.

4 Repeat two or three times.

5 Next, breathe in and raise your head and tailbone.

6 Breathe out, bringing the spine back to a neutral position.

7 Repeat two or three times.

8 Now combine the front and back stretches with your exhalations and inhalations, raising your head and tailbone as you breathe in, and dropping your head and tailbone as you breathe out. Repeat two or three times.

BACKBENDS

Backbends are particularly challenging and are best accomplished when you have stabilized the lower back by engaging the abdominal muscles. Practise this before attempting the backbend postures of yoga, and follow the backbends with full pranamasana and bhekasana (see opposite).

When you do backbends, whether standing or kneeling, the weight should be released down through the point of contact with the floor. Once the whole body is releasing its weight downwards, slowly draw up the muscles of the pelvic floor towards the navel (this is similar to a yoga breathing exercise known as mulabandha – see page 113). As you draw these muscles up, you will feel the front of your torso lengthening. Go with this lengthening and maintain this lift in the pelvic floor muscles. Let your back arch backwards slowly, being careful not to go beyond the natural limit your body will place on you.

1 Go onto your knees and place your hands on your lower back, with the fingers resting on the buttocks.

2 Breathe in, and as you breathe out draw up the abdominal and pelvic floor muscles, and feel them taking the support of the lower back.

3 Maintain this contraction as you slowly continue to lengthen the front of the spine, leaning back while you breathe in.

4 Hold for one complete inhalation and exhalation, and then release.

FULL PRANAMASANA

This is a good counter-stretch to do once you have completed your backbend stretches. It releases the tension from the lower back and opens the shoulders.

1 Drop back onto your heels (place a folded blanket under your buttocks if this feels too uncomfortable).

2 Stretch your arms forwards and let your forearms and forehead rest on the floor.

3 Remain in this posture for four or five conscious breaths, breathing into your back and being aware of the movement in your back as you breathe.

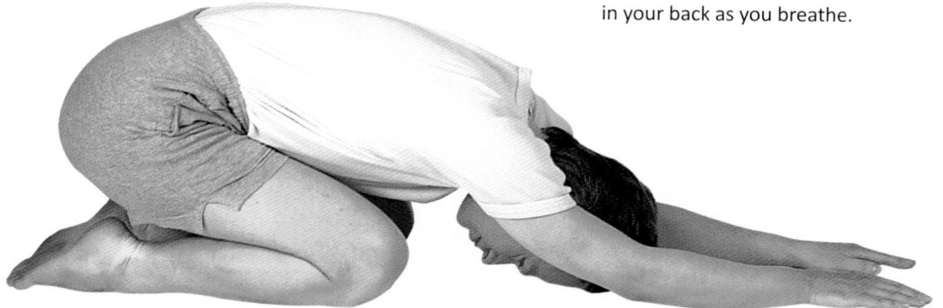

BHEKASANA

This is another good way to open the hips and shoulders. In this posture, it's important to release the weight of the pelvis down through the legs.

1 Sit back on your heels and spread your knees as far apart as you can.

2 Breathe in, and as you breathe out slowly release down, placing your forehead and forearms on the floor.

3 Keep releasing down as you hold the posture, remaining for four or five conscious breaths.

MUSCLE ENERGY TECHNIQUE

A particularly useful technique to employ in stretching is MET – muscle energy technique. It involves using the energy of the muscle to help take it through especially stubborn resistance. The origins of MET are in physiotherapy and osteopathy – disciplines that both use it. If you incorporate MET wisely in your yoga practice, without losing mindfulness, you will find it very beneficial.

I recommend to everyone engaging in or teaching yoga Leon Chaitow's book *Muscle Energy Techniques* (see page 141 for details). In this book, he quotes Philip Greenman, a professor of biomechanics, on the MET technique:

> *Muscle energy techniques can be used to lengthen a shortened, contractured or spastic muscle; to strengthen a physiologically weakened muscle or group of muscles; to reduce localized edema, to relieve passive congestion and to mobilize an articulation with restricted mobility.*

With MET offering such a wide range of applications, it would be negligent to ignore it in our yoga practice. Yoga has never shied away from incorporating what is beneficial to its purpose.

HOW IT WORKS

In the muscle energy technique, the restricted muscle is first taken into a contraction and then, following the contraction, gently and slowly stretched. A muscle that's held in a slight contraction for about ten seconds will go into an immediate relaxation for about twenty seconds after it has been released. This process is accomplished via the nervous system. This is a particularly good time to allow the muscle to stretch and reach a new resistance barrier.

When contracting the muscle, it's best not to push as hard as you can, but to use only about ten per cent of your strength. Doing this means that you will involve more and more muscle fibre as the contraction is held, rather than only involving the muscle fibres that are habitually pressed into action.

When a physiotherapist or osteopath practises MET on a patient, they will act as an 'operator' to assist the patient. I have adapted the technique so that it can be used without the assistance of someone else – so you can use it in your yoga practice when you are on your own. A way of using MET to release the hamstrings in preparation for paschimottanasana (back extension posture – see page 70) is shown on the page opposite, as an example of how the technique works. You can use MET when you are stretching any of the muscles in the body – the principle remains the same.

LENGTHENING THE HAMSTRINGS

Tightness in the hamstrings can cause not only back pain but also headaches. To use MET to help lengthen the resistant hamstrings try the following:

1 Sit with your legs stretched out in front of you. Bring up one leg, placing the heel on the floor, lining up midway up the calf of the opposite leg.

2 Wrap your hands around the back of your thigh so that they are in contact with the hamstrings.

3 Breathe in and, as you breathe out, with about ten per cent of your strength push your heel down into the floor – not down towards the other foot. You will feel the hamstrings under your hand engaging. (Don't use more than about ten per cent of your strength for this contraction. If you engage your full strength you will engage only those muscle fibres conditioned to responding. If you engage the minimal strength to the contraction, more and more of the muscle fibres will become involved in the contraction and so engaged in the subsequent stretch.)

4 Hold this contraction for a slow count of ten and then release.

5 Breathe in and wrap your hands around your instep (or use a strap, as shown above, if you are unable to reach).

6 As you breathe out, slowly straighten your leg.

7 Hold this stretch for about fifteen seconds, keeping your breathing regular, then release.

8 Repeat with the other leg.

YOGA AND THE FIVE FORCES

Emanating from the One Supreme Self
Came earth, water, fire, air and space –
These five constitute both the seen
And the unseen of all bodies:
From Brahma through to human beings,
Nature and even solid rock –
Are all pervaded by these five,
And through these five
Each is allocated its own nature.

THE UDDHAVA GITA, DIALOGUE 16, VERSE 5,
translated by Swami Ambikananda Saraswati

The system of yoga that was finally codified by the great sage Patanjali as the *Yoga Sutras* became known as ashtanga yoga (eight-limbed yoga) or raja yoga ('the sovereign path of yoga'). Its eight 'limbs' or parts are detailed below.

1 **ĀSANA** (yoga posture)
2 **PRĀṆĀYĀMA** (control of the vitality, usually through conscious breathing)
3 **YAMA** (maintaining a certain set of values in your dealings with others, which includes non-violence, truthfulness, not stealing, lack of greed and the conservation of energy in order to direct it to Brahman, the divine)
4 **NIYAMA** (maintaining certain disciplines in your own life, including cleanliness, contentment, self-study, a simple ascetic lifestyle and remaining present to the indwelling presence, Ishvara)
5 **PRATYĀHĀRA** (withdrawal of the senses from external stimuli)
6 **DHĀRĀṆĀ** (single-minded concentration)
7 **DHYĀNA** (meditation)
8 **SAMĀDHI** (the experience of freedom from bondage)

When the great sage Patanjali referred to 'asana', he was not in fact speaking of the variety of postures we find in hatha yoga. He was speaking only of being seated and being able to maintain that seated posture, without moving, for the duration of the time of meditation. Only then is it possible to introduce the 'monkey-mind' to the lofty notion of a life beyond our immediate situation. Only when we are able to be seated without discomfort or pain to distract us can we take the next steps on the road to freedom – the steps of withdrawal of our attention, focused concentration and, finally, that absorbed meditation in which the ecstasy of freedom becomes a possibility.

Anyone who has tried to sit motionless will know how difficult it is: perhaps you get an itch, then your knees ache so you shift a little, then you need to adjust your back, then you get another itch, and so on. What is it that prevents us from holding a quiet and comfortable seated posture? The prana isn't flowing freely through the nadis and the gunas are disturbed, and this resonates through the tattvas and echoes through all five 'sheaths' or koshas.

To bring about this free flow, and move closer towards the perfection of health, happiness and quality of life, we need the practices of hatha yoga: asanas, pranayama, mudras (gestures with the hands) and bandhas (locked positions). We also need the power of mantras, a controlled mind and a diet that is conducive to all these practices. This section is devoted to these aspects and their impact on the tattvas – and, hence, your life.

About the FIVE TATTVAS

ĀKĀŚA TATTVA
VIṢUDDHA CHAKRA

VAYU TATTVA
ANĀHATA CHAKRA

What begins to emerge is that for the yogis, the unseen world – which they called *avyakta* – was as important as the seen world, *vyakta*. The panchatattva – space, air, fire, water and earth – belong to the unseen world, and could not be perceived through the senses. While we are unable to directly see any of these tattvas, we experience their effects.

The panchatattva work on certain atoms to cause them to create molecules that become space in the visible world – the space that was created with the 'big bang', and in which this universe moved from a state of chaos to form stars and planets moving in determined orbits. There is also the inner space in which our thoughts, emotions and ideas find the space to exist. Similarly, this potential power works on atoms and even subatomic matter to form movement – the movement of an atmosphere with winds and hurricanes, and the movement of the signals travelling along nerves and thoughts flashing through our consciousness. Continuing in this way, the potential power 'creates' the fires of the universe – the bright suns furiously burning and heating and warming the planets close to them, as well as the fire here on earth.

This potential became the ability within us to transform. The foods we eat are metamorphosed into glycogen, and then transformed again into glucose. Then, in every cell of our bodies, this glucose is burned in the presence of oxygen and transformed into energy and carbon dioxide. We transform information into ideas, philosophies and concepts. When this potential acts on matter in a different way, it becomes the vast oceans of our planet and the interstitial fluid, blood plasma, saliva and urinary fluid within us. It also becomes the waters of the womb in which new life is formed and our active and pervasive creative talents that ebb and flow though our whole body. And, finally, it acts to create the solid ground for these others to rest on – the mountains, hills and plains, and the earth beneath our feet. Within us, it's the solid mountain of bone and the supportive and nurturing side of our nature.

Each panchatattva will act differently in each of us – just as we see them acting differently within nature. For example, the 'effect' of Akasha Tattva (space), with its power of emergence and initiation, may vary slightly from person to person. If Akasha Tattva becomes particularly *rajasic* (overactive) in me, I experience it as a desire to tidy up and immediately begin clearing out my cupboard. (Unfortunately, this state seldom lasts for the duration of the job and I end up pushing everything back into the cupboard in much the same haphazard state that it was in originally!) Someone in whom Agni Tattva (fire) is predominant might experience the ascendancy of Akasha Tattva (space) as a desire to reorganize their environment in some way – to paint the house or buy new curtains or furniture, perhaps, or reorganize their social schedule. Whatever our own

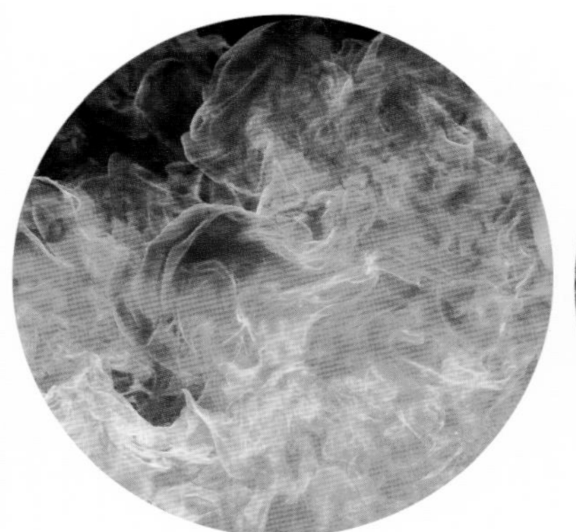

AGNI TATTVA
MAṆIPŪRA CHAKRA

APAS TATTVA
SVĀDHIṢṬHĀNA CHAKRA

PṚTHVI TATTVA
MŪLĀDHĀRA CHAKRA

predominant tattva may be, Akasha Tattva will always provide the capacity to organize or reorganize some part of our life – to tidy things up. If someone's predominant tattva is Akasha itself, that person will by nature be someone who always has order in their life, likes to colour-code cupboards and likes a place for everything (and everything in its place!).

OBSERVING YOUR PATTERNS

The fun of this model is observing yourself closely and honestly enough to judge correctly the hierarchy of the tattvas expressed in your actual experience – rather than assuming that your predominant tattva is the one you are most attracted to. There's also the challenge of daily and hourly observation as we go about our everyday lives, to see how the balance of the tattvas within us changes as the day goes by.

The people we see, the tasks we engage in, the conversations we have, the environment we frequent and the foods we eat will all have an impact on the tattvas. For instance, I'm a great lover of coffee, and three or four mugs a week has no detrimental impact on the free flow of prana through the koshas. However, as soon as I go over that amount it seems to agitate Vayu Tattva (air) into a particularly rajasic state. This expresses itself in me as agitation and impatience. My body becomes 'dry' and dehydrated, and I have to rub masses of moisturizer into my skin. It took me years to realize that it was the slightly bitter and delicious hot brown liquid that I used to pour down my throat all day that was having this effect!

True health

As we become aware of these changes, we can adapt our yoga practices to compensate accordingly and maintain a free flow of prana throughout the body and throughout our lives. What we need to discern as we explore patterns and expressions in ourselves is not only the pattern of tattvas, and which is predominant, but also when one of them has become *tamasic* (stagnant) or rajasic. What we are seeking is a sattvic – balanced – state through all of the tattvas in which the prana is flowing freely through the nadis.

This may not mean that we remain 'disease-free' all our lives. It certainly doesn't mean that we won't ever die – as soon as we are born, the yogis observed, death becomes certain. However, it does mean having a greater awareness of what is happening behind the appearance of 'disease' and discomfort in our body, and being better able to support and adapt our lives and yoga practice to these changes. In this capacity lies true health: we maintain wholeness, integrity and perfection, regardless of the changes in our circumstances. We allow all the different parts of the self to participate in the whole and, in turn, each part to care for the whole.

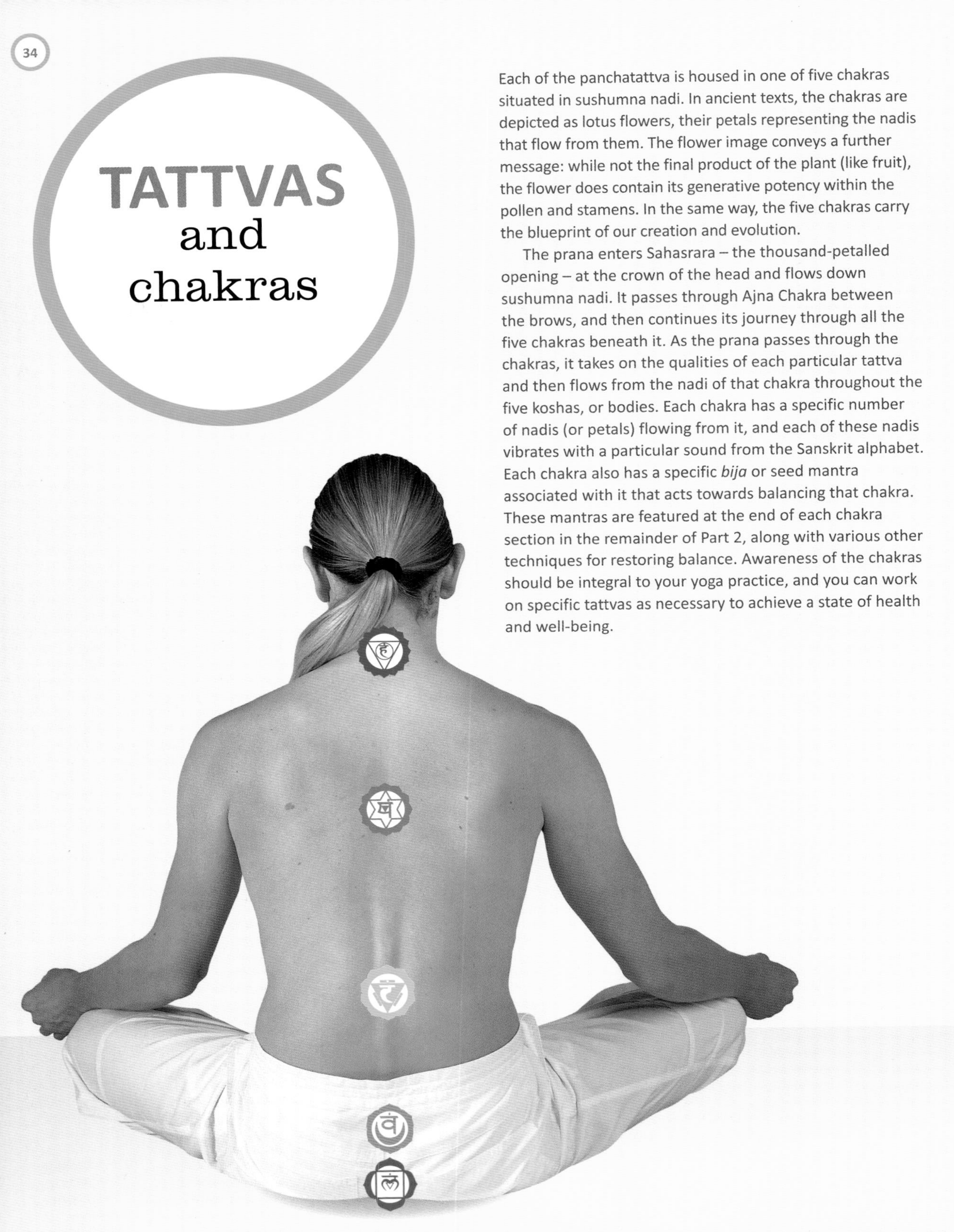

TATTVAS and chakras

Each of the panchatattva is housed in one of five chakras situated in sushumna nadi. In ancient texts, the chakras are depicted as lotus flowers, their petals representing the nadis that flow from them. The flower image conveys a further message: while not the final product of the plant (like fruit), the flower does contain its generative potency within the pollen and stamens. In the same way, the five chakras carry the blueprint of our creation and evolution.

The prana enters Sahasrara – the thousand-petalled opening – at the crown of the head and flows down sushumna nadi. It passes through Ajna Chakra between the brows, and then continues its journey through all the five chakras beneath it. As the prana passes through the chakras, it takes on the qualities of each particular tattva and then flows from the nadi of that chakra throughout the five koshas, or bodies. Each chakra has a specific number of nadis (or petals) flowing from it, and each of these nadis vibrates with a particular sound from the Sanskrit alphabet. Each chakra also has a specific *bija* or seed mantra associated with it that acts towards balancing that chakra. These mantras are featured at the end of each chakra section in the remainder of Part 2, along with various other techniques for restoring balance. Awareness of the chakras should be integral to your yoga practice, and you can work on specific tattvas as necessary to achieve a state of health and well-being.

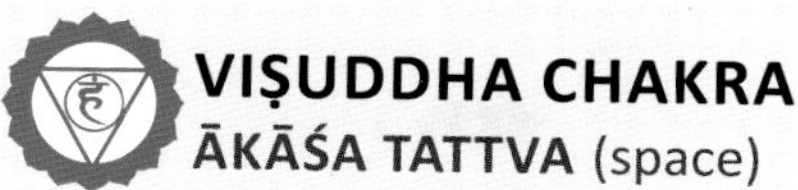

VIṢUDDHA CHAKRA
ĀKĀŚA TATTVA (space)

- At the base of the throat

This is the beginning of coming into being. In the centre of this chakra is the orb of the luminescent and full moon, the sign of space, showering its cooling nectar throughout the five bodies via the nadis. The prana flows from its sixteen smoky-coloured petals.

KEYWORDS: integrity • judgement • attention

SVĀDHIṢṬHĀNA CHAKRA
APAS TATTVA (water)

- Behind the base of the spine

Our most potent creative powers lie within this chakra. In its dark blue-black watery centre rests the water sign – a silvery crescent moon. The prana flows from six petals, which take on a vermilion hue as they radiate from the centre.

KEYWORDS: creativity • fluidity • perception

ANĀHATA CHAKRA
VAYU TATTVA (air)

- Behind the heart

Here, the full force of intention moves from potential to actual. In the centre of the deep-red Anahata lotus is the smoky hexagon – the sign of air – and above it is a light more radiant than ten million lightning flashes. The prana flows from its twelve golden petals.

KEYWORDS: movement • impulse • sensitivity

MŪLĀDHĀRA CHAKRA
PṚTHVI TATTVA (earth)

- At the perineum

Here lies the call 'to be' – our destiny and the realization of our potential. Sushumna nadi is rooted here, and the sacred and mysterious psychic force known as kundalini slumbers in this chakra, wound around the lingam form of Shiva. In its centre is the sign of earth, a yellow square, and the prana flows from its four blood-red petals.

KEYWORDS: stability • cohesion • synthesis

MAṆIPŪRA CHAKRA
AGNI TATTVA (fire)

- Behind the navel

This chakra holds the power of transformation. In the centre of the chakra, which is the colour of a dark rain cloud, rests the fire sign – the blazing triangle with its apex facing downwards. The prana flows from its ten bright-yellow petals.

KEYWORDS: transformation • alchemy • vision

ENLIGHTENMENT

As we discovered on page 17, winding in a double helix around sushumna nadi are ida nadi and pingala nadi. These end in Ajna Chakra at the root of the nose and form the granthi, or knots, that kundalini – once awakened – must break through on the journey to unite with Shiva in Sahasrara, at the crown of the head. This journey represents the spiritual aspirant's passage towards enlightenment, and the final uniting of kundalini and Shiva is the moment of enlightenment.

Situated at the base of the throat, Vishuddha Chakra is the focal point of Akasha Tattva – the power of space. This is the prana transforming wave to particle – the beginning of coming into being. It has no substance and yet it occupies all substances. It's the cellular wisdom coded into the strands of DNA and RNA locked in the cells of the body. It's the space occupied by every cell and every body, and it's the space between them – whether they are bodies in the same room or galaxies in space. It's the epitome of order and refinement. There's a wonderful Sanskrit word that Patanjali uses to begin his sutras: *atha*. It's known as one of the auspicious sounds, and although usually translated as 'now' it's a pregnant 'now', filled with possibility and intention. In this chakra, Akasha Tattva is that charged potential. It's the very first vibration of prana as the intention to create.

VIŞUDDHA CHAKRA

the power of space

PRANIC PHASE

Prana is described as passing through five phases in the process of its flow. This universal vitality connects us with the outer limits of creation and invokes the universal being each time we breathe in – the inhalation being the first of the five phases of prana. Prana is both vitality and this first breath. The human form is called *Ishvarapuram*, the walled city of Ishvara. In a lotus floating in the centre of the heart, Ishvara is said to reside as the *pranabrahman* – ruler of the body and its vitality. Each 'next breath', or next prana, is taken under its auspices. And it's under the auspices of Vishuddha Chakra that our independent life begins with that first breath. We aren't yet fully formed, we haven't yet come to our full potential – but we have begun the journey here when we take that first breath. It's the impulse that becomes the tug on the crura of the diaphragm, causing it to descend, and the inhalation to begin.

EFFECT ON MIND AND BODY

Vishuddha governs our sense of hearing. It's the ability of our whole being to listen to our true nature and to act on its whispered wisdom. For all of us, life began in the darkness of unknowing – in the deep passageways of the fallopian tubes, where two independent cells merged their creative energies to form new life. From this point on, our lives depend on the individual cells and on the body maintaining their integrity. Failure in this maintenance signals a loss of vitality in Vishuddha Chakra, and that it has gone into a tamasic state. As our cells lose their integrity, our mental processes become confused about who we are and what our true purpose is. As the chakra struggles to regain strength, we might find ourselves indulging in ritualized order that has nothing to do with the refining of matter that is the true power of Akasha. An overly rajasic Vishuddha Chakra can cause us to become rigid and stiff as we distort the extraordinary sense of order of this chakra into habitual and compulsive behaviour, indulging in the futility of trying to impose 'non-change' on our world of constant change (order dislikes the chaos of change).

THIS CHAKRA IN ASCENDANCY

If you are someone in whom this chakra has a natural ascendancy, you will always seek order in your world. Neatness and order won't place a discipline on you – you will be naturally inclined to them. You will find that you live your life by certain principles, and that deviating from them causes you disturbance. You will have a gift for working out systems, whatever the field – whether in computers, cleaning or government. It will always be important to you that people live up to their obligations – even the obligation of something as seemingly trivial as arriving on time for meetings. You don't like surprises – even pleasant ones. You are most comfortable when you can predict the outcome of a certain set of events. You may experience some difficulties letting go of things that have come into your life, but when you do cut the tie it's with finality and precision, and you never look back.

ESSENTIAL ĀKĀŚA TYPE

The essential Akasha type is the pandit performing prescribed ritual. No detail is left out: the sequence of movements, sounds and gestures follows a perfect and seamless order. The ritual isn't questioned – it's adhered to and its disciplines welcomed. Performing the separate elements of the ritual, the pandit brings its elements together to create a symmetrical pattern with graceful accuracy. The Akasha person is one for whom order and accuracy are of primary importance. Each situation will be addressed by separating it into distinct tasks.

NAṬARĀJĀSANA I

This posture comes from the ancient *murthi* (form) of Shiva as he dances the dance of creation (this form is given the name Nataraj). From its chaos, with his matted locks flying in every direction and surrounded by fire, the order of the dance emerges. The whole universe is this dance of Shiva – everything is breaking down, falling apart, transforming, rebuilding. But we resist these forces of change. Ignoring change as the supreme law of this universe, we attempt to cling to what is – and in that lies all our pain. We seek to measure, to limit the limitless – but that is also the nature of creation: the undefined becomes defined. The order of creation lies in the chaos of the dance.

It's this process of manifestation and ceaseless change that's depicted in this first Nataraj pose. It requires perfect balance and full attention from the practitioner. As you assume the pose – which looks deceptively simple – watch that your breath remains non-reactive. If you become aware that you are holding your breath, relax and allow the breath to flow.

- Stand in simple standing pose (tadasana – see pranamasana on page 40).
- Move your right foot forwards and place the foot down with the toes pointing out (two o'clock position). Bend the right knee and take all of your weight over your right leg, ensuring that the head is aligned with the right heel.
- Breathe in, and as you breathe out lift your left leg and bring it into position in front of the right leg.
- At the same time, move your arms into position.
- Hold the posture while you keep the breath flowing. Be aware of all the dynamic movement within your body as you hold the posture still and steady. Go deep into the inner self and sense the stillness within the movement.

ŪRDHVA BHUJAÑGĀSANA

Raised cobra posture

Having allowed the hips complete release in vajrasana (see opposite), they are now opened and strengthened in bhujangasana. Many of the yoga postures are named after animals. The yogis were obviously keen observers of their environment and would have been particularly aware of the cobra, held to be sacred to Shiva, the god of yoga. In raised cobra posture the lower half of the body becomes the support of the upper half, which acts like the raised cobra's hood. Once the position is adopted, there's that sense of 'atha' – the auspicious moment. It isn't waiting or expectancy – although it stirs feelings similar to both – but is rather dynamic awareness, the moment of Akasha Tattva.

Before you begin this exercise, you should do some of the stretches that open the 'front' of the back (see 'Warming up', pages 25–6).

- Go onto all fours, knees hip distance apart and heels of the hands under the shoulders.
- Take a step back with one leg and then the other, and support the weight of the body on the toes, which are tucked under, and the hands.
- Breathe in, and as you breathe out release your hips until your legs are parallel to the floor.

Once you are in the final posture don't let your shoulders come up around your ears. Let your shoulder blades push down your back. Neither should you allow the back of the neck to become crushed or shortened. Let the muscles there keep lengthening and releasing. Hold for two or three breaths and release.

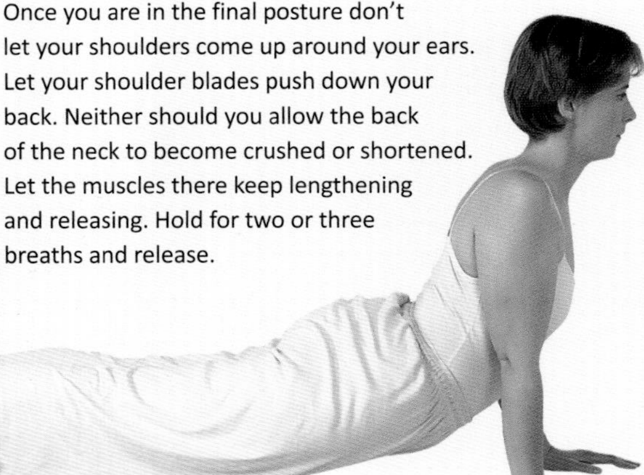

VAJRĀSANA

Thunderbolt posture

Vajra means 'thunderbolt', specifically the thunderbolt that's the weapon of the god Indra, ruler of heaven. It's a sacred weapon, and as such is one used to slay our most potent enemy – the one within. The enemy manifests itself in those internal judgements that make us feel inadequate and inhibit our potential. As you sit and watch the thoughts drifting through your consciousness, observe these thoughts. Try not to let your attention wander off after any thought, nor attempt to suppress any thought. The power of this posture is observation. We know from quantum physics that observation impacts on that which is being observed. It's through the power of this observation that we are restored to wholeness. This sentiment was first expressed by the sage Patanjali more than two thousand years ago as:

Yogaś chitta-vṛtti-nirodhaḥ

Yoga is the stilling of the movement of thought in consciousness.

YOGA SUTRAS, CHAPTER 1, VERSE 2

Akasha Tattva contains the creative potential of any moment or mass. It's movement from chaos to order. Before beginning an Akasha sequence of asanas, adopt Vajrasana (see right). Rest your hands on your thighs, palms facing down. (If your knees feel uncomfortable, place a folded towel under your buttocks.) In this posture the ligaments supporting the hip joint become perfectly relaxed, and the muscles of the lower back are able to release better. While maintaining the posture, let your gaze rest on the floor about four feet in front of you and follow the directions given to the right.

- Release your weight down through the sitting bones, which are resting on your heels. Your heels should be hip distance apart with the big toes touching.
- Let your weight continue down through the feet and into the floor.
- Allow your spine to flow upwards.
- Let your shoulders release and widen, and let the muscles at the back of your neck lengthen.
- As the shoulders widen and the neck lengthens, feel the neck opening and energizing.

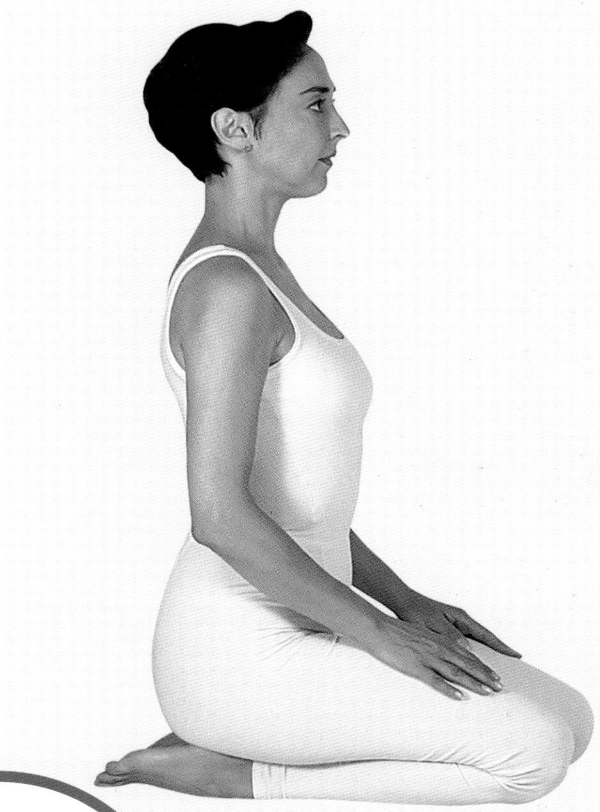

CAUTION

If you suffer from varicose veins or problems with your knees, don't sit directly on your heels. Place a small meditation stool or folded rug under your buttocks.

PRANAMĀSANA I

The posture of greeting

Our first moment of meeting – whether a person, or a new day or situation – is the moment that contains all the potential of what is to follow. Yet, rather than bringing full consciousness to it, we easily slide past, directly to contact. Pranamasana gives us the opportunity to recognize that moment.

Begin in standing pose, tadasana. The body's inner wisdom knows how to stand up straight, but we interfere with this by placing tensions in muscles instead of allowing a natural muscle tone to emerge.

1 Stand in tadasana, with your feet hip distance apart so as not to create tension in the lower back and buttocks. Let your arms release down to the side, with the shoulders widening. Feel that your head is perfectly balanced between your heels. Allow your weight to flow down through your body, legs and feet into the ground. Don't try to 'pull up'. As you release your weight down, you will become aware of the energy flow up through the body and through the back to the crown of the head. Observe this down–up flow of forces.

2 Breathe in, and as you breathe out bring the palms of your hands together over your heart. Feel the palms touching and the energy of Akasha Tattva descending into the heart, where it becomes movement. Now allow your attention to flow outwards, greeting everything in your field of vision. Hold the posture and the attitude of greetings for a few breaths before releasing.

ŚIRṢĀSANA

Headstand posture

The headstand posture is probably the most recognizable of all yoga postures. In this and the other inverted postures the prana is prevented from flowing down sushumna nadi and gathers in the throat and head area – adding to the vitality of Akasha Tattva.

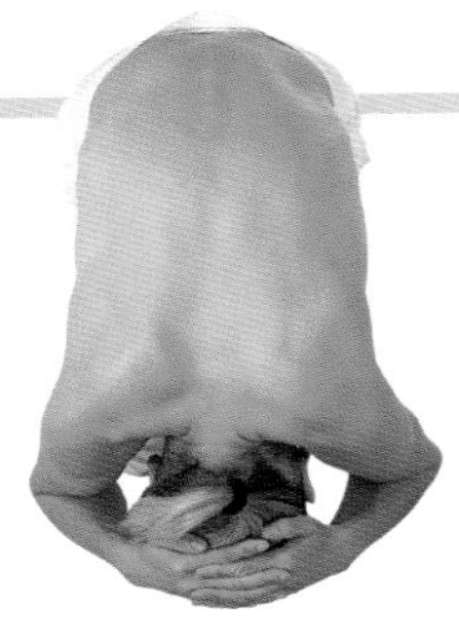

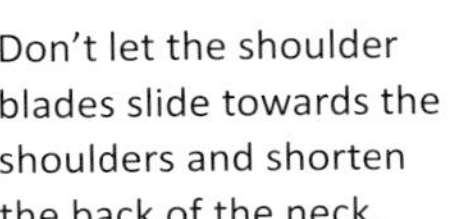

Don't let the shoulder blades slide towards the shoulders and shorten the back of the neck.

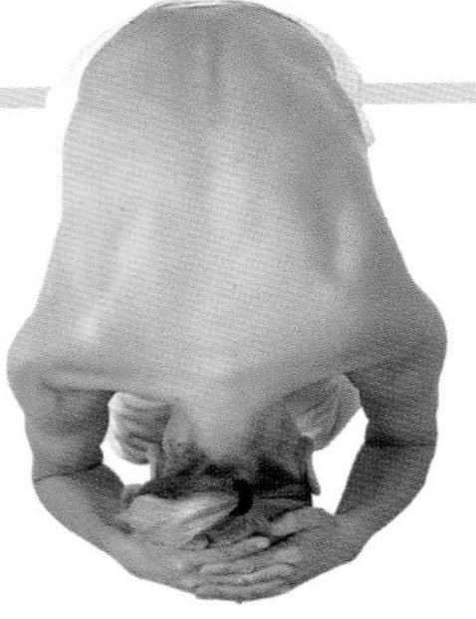

Ensure that you keep the back open and strong and the muscles at the back of the neck lengthened.

1 Sit in vajrasana (see page 39) and, leaning forwards, place your left forearm on the ground, extended out in front of you. Place the other elbow on the ground, with the fingers resting on the forearm of the extended arm. This will give you a measurement for the distance of the arms.

CONTRAINDICATIONS

If you suffer from any of the following conditions, consult your health practitioner for advice before attempting inversion postures:

- High blood pressure. While the flow of blood to the brain is kept constant, even during inversion, your own physician should be contacted for advice prior to any practice.
- Glaucoma or detached retina. The blood vessels of the eye become engorged during inversions and could worsen the condition.
- Disc problems in your neck or thoracic vertebrae, particularly cervical spondylitis; reduced disc space in the vertebrae of the neck or arthritis in the cervical vertebrae. In an inversion posture the weight of the body is taken through the neck.

CAUTION

As with any posture, if you feel discomfort release the posture immediately. There's no gain from pain in yoga. The aim is to increase body consciousness.

2 Bring the right hand out to meet the left hand. Place the crown of your head on the ground, with the back of the head resting against your interlocked fingers. This will give you a measurement for the distance of the arms.

3 Breathe in and tuck your toes under. Breathe out and push up, straightening your legs. Slowly walk towards your head, breathing freely. Continue this walking, taking small steps until you feel the point of balance when the hips are over the shoulders.

4 Once you have felt the point of balance, slowly begin to raise your legs, bending the knees. Don't try to 'kick up'. That's wasted effort. Stay patient and work on the posture. Over time, as your confidence grows, you will find that moment of perfect balance, even in this inverted position.

5 Straighten your legs and let them flow up, allowing your heels to align above your head. Hold the posture, breathing with awareness, for as long as is comfortable, then release by bending the knees and slowly lowering the feet to the floor. Never sit up directly after the posture – go into shankhasana (see page 89) for a few moments, observing your breath before coming up.

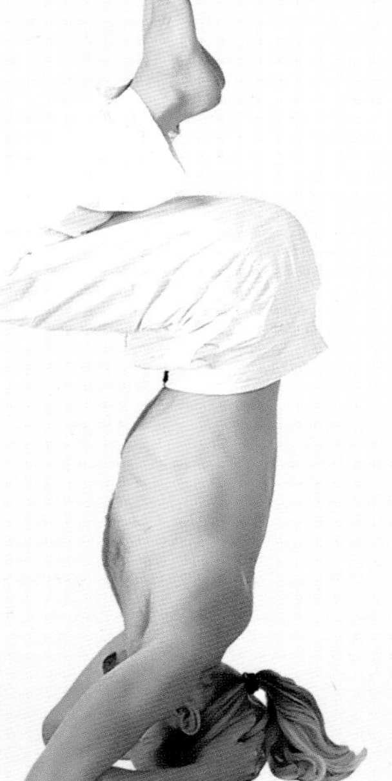

SARVĀNGĀSANA

Whole body posture

Sarva means 'whole' or 'entire', and *anga* is 'a limb' or 'the body'. In this asana the whole body is supported by the hands, arms and shoulders as it goes into an inversion posture. Only one inversion is mentioned in the ancient text on hatha yoga, the *Hatha Yoga Pradipika*: viparit karani (see page 81). One of the unique features of hatha yoga as a bodywork system is its use of inverted postures. In these postures, we are able to reverse the normally deleterious effects of gravity on the body as we use its force to reverse its effects.

In this posture, Vishuddha Chakra at the base of the cervical vertebrae (the vertebrae of the neck) is opened and energized. It also allows the flow of lymph fluid to drain quickly from the lower extremities and pelvis, thus having a wonderful detoxifying effect on the body.

INVERTED POSTURES AND WOMEN

Much has been made of inversions and women, with claims that the inversions are either outdated (that they can be a cause of endometriosis, for example), or downright silly (that they cause uterine cancer). Yoga emerged and evolved within Hinduism, and in that culture, during menstruation, women are prohibited from doing certain tasks such as cooking or entering the temple. I suspect, and my guru Swami Venkatesananda certainly believed, that this prohibition on inversions during menstruation was a cultural bias – the shoulderstand and headstand being considered the 'king' and 'queen' of yoga postures. Swamiji advised me that women would have to recognize that, while in its most ancient history hatha yoga was probably

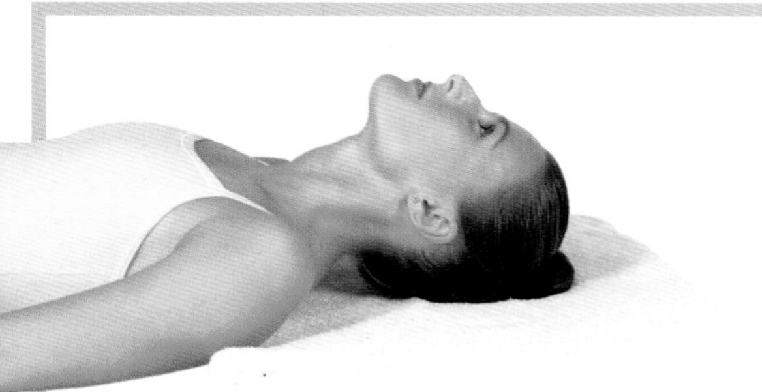

WATCHPOINT When you lie down, ensure that the back of your head is resting on the floor and that the back of the neck isn't shortened and crunched like this.

1 Lie down on your back with your arms flat on the ground at your sides. Breathe in, and as you breathe out bend your knees and bring your thighs towards your abdomen. Engaging the muscles of the back and abdomen, give your bottom a lift, away from the floor.

CAUTION

If the muscles of your neck and shoulders feel uncomfortably tight, don't attempt this posture – instead, do some of the forward bends like paschimottanasana (see page 70) to help lengthen and release neck and shoulder muscles. Until the muscles in your neck have lengthened through repeated practice, place a folded rug under your shoulders, making your shoulders slightly higher than your head.

practised by women alongside men, in its more modern use it had become a male preserve. Now that women were practising hatha yoga, they should investigate for themselves what is appropriate to women.

In that spirit of enquiry we found that endometriosis (a condition in which cells that are usually found inside the uterus form and grow in the pelvic cavity outside of the uterus) isn't caused by 'retrograde' menstruation, in which the blood flows back into the fallopian tubes. Research now tells us that it's caused by the growth of cells in the pelvis outside of the uterus behaving like uterine lining cells and growing on the outside walls of the uterus. While it's true that the blood vessels of the lining of the uterus are very thin and can rupture easily, this can occur whether we are standing on our feet or our head.

Given the above, I would like to offer the following advice to women:

- If you suffer from heavy periods, avoid inversions during the days of the heaviest flow, and, if it brings relief, rest your pelvis on some folded blankets with your legs up against a wall. This assists the flow of lymph from the engorged area.
- Allow your own experience to lead you. Yoga has always been an experience-based system, with personal experience taking precedence over injunctions. If the shoulderstand brings relief and doesn't cause a heavier flow of blood, continue doing it.

CONTRAINDICATIONS

All the contraindications of the headstand also apply to the shoulderstand (see page 41).

2 As soon as you are able, place your hands on your lower back and begin to straighten your legs.

3 Once you are in the final posture, allow the muscles of your face, scalp and neck to release. Observe your breathing in this posture – it will feel very different. The abdominal cavity is now resting on the thoracic cavity, reducing its space, so breathing will be happening in the upper chest and the blood will be flowing there, nourishing the upper part of the lungs. While you hold the posture, ensure that you release your weight down through the shoulders. Feel that the collarbone is lengthening – helping the shoulders to release into the ground and widen.

MATSYĀSANA
Fish posture

This posture resembles the body of a large fish as it breaks the surface of water and then disappears back down. The whole front of the body and spine are lengthened, opened and lifted against gravity. When released, the prana of Vishuddha Chakra, carrying the organization of Akasha Tattva, flows freely downwards.

BREATHING DURING MATSYASANA

The power of gravity means that there's more blood for oxygen exchange in the lower part of the lungs. In sarvangasana, the previous pose (see pages 42–3), this effect is reversed and the upper part of the lungs receive a generous supply of blood. If you use matsyasana as the counterpose for sarvangasana, you open the top of the lungs, which have already been suffused with blood.

WATCHPOINT Because this posture opens the front of the spine and takes the neck into an extreme extension, give your body time to adapt to this unusual stretch. This may be particularly necessary if your job requires you to sit at a desk all day or if you do a lot of driving. Lie flat on the floor and place a bolster or rolled blanket underneath your shoulder blades. Allow the back of the head to rest on the floor, and just enjoy the sensations of the front of the body opening.

MATSAYASANA WITH STRAIGHT LEGS

1 Extend your legs out in front of you and place your hands on the floor behind you, with your fingertips just under your buttocks. Slowly lower yourself onto your elbows. During this sequence, keep the muscles at the back of the neck strong and lengthened.

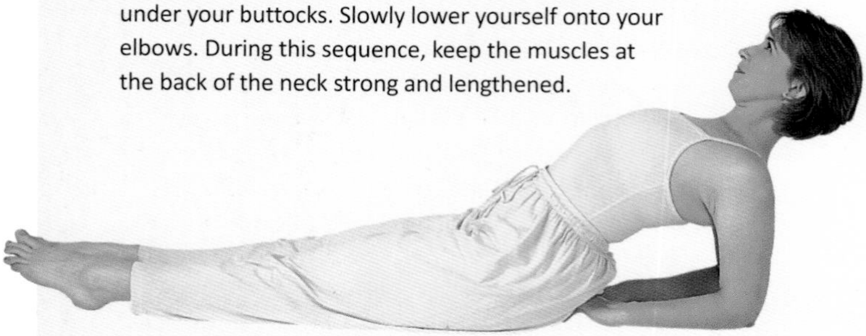

2 Slowly move your elbows out of the way and release the muscles at the back of the neck, allowing the head to go back, maintaining control rather than allowing it to drop back. Lower yourself onto the crown of your head by continuing to move the arms out of the way.

3 Either let your arms remain resting by your side, letting the shoulders drop back and the collarbone lengthen, or bring the palms together over your heart, creating a mudra that acts to enhance the flow of prana in the upper body.

Allow yourself, while holding and breathing in this posture, to breathe into the upper part of the chest and feel the full power and capacity of the muscles between the ribs (the intercostal muscles) for expansion.

MATSYASANA AND ASTHMA

Asthma is a very typical condition of prana remaining concentrated in the upper part of the body and not descending properly. Simple matsyasana, with the legs straight, practised by anyone suffering from asthma, will not only allow the muscles that have tightened around the bronchioles, and thus restricted the air passageway, to release and open, but will allow for a descent of prana on release of the posture.

CONTRAINDICATIONS

This is one of the postures to avoid during pregnancy, as it places enormous strain on the womb. Any difficulties or pain in the neck should also be a warning that you aren't yet ready for this posture and need to work on lengthening and opening the back of the neck with forward bends.

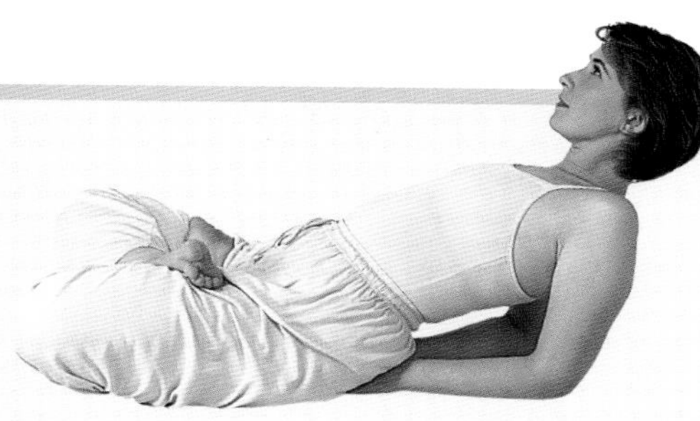

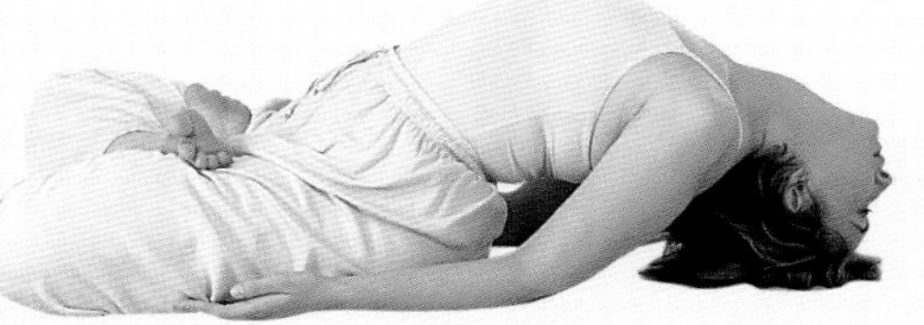

COUNTERPOSE

The counterpose for any given posture is generally the easiest pose opposite to the direction of the strain, the idea being to stretch and strengthen the body in the opposite direction. When we do a deep forward-bending posture, for example, the counterpose that compensates is a gentle backward-bending posture. And when we do a deep backbend, the counterpose would be a gentle forward bend. This provides the body with all that it needs to reorganize itself around these movements. If you can find out where the strain is, from that you can decide on an appropriate counterpose – remeber that the counterpose for a given posture is not always the same for every person. Matsyasana offers a possibility of a counterpose for sarvangasana. However, it's also a powerful posture in its own right. After completing matsyasana it's good to adopt shankhasana (see page 89) as a counterpose for a few breaths.

MATSYASANA IN PADMASANA

1 Adopting padmasana (see page 93) during matsyasana enhances the stretch and opens the pelvic area. If you are perfectly comfortable in padmasana, you may attempt this powerful stretch. The instructions for going into it are very much the same as with the legs straight. Go into padmasana, then place your hands behind you, fingertips under your buttocks. Lean back on to your elbows. Your legs will lift off the floor – don't be concerned, as there's time to release them once you are in the completed posture.

2 Slowly let your head release backwards and, gently sliding your arms out, lower yourself onto the crown of your head.

3 Release your arms and either let them rest on the floor beside you, allowing your shoulders to drop back, or place the palms together over your heart.

NILAYANA PADMĀSANA

Descending lotus posture

The tattvas at the two opposite ends of the spectrum are Akasha (space) and Prithvi (earth). Akasha is the vitality before it begins movement towards actualization and form, while Prithvi is the prana in its most manifest state. Yet both of these respond well to balancing postures. The moment of balance – when we are organizing ourselves around gravity on one foot, or even the ball of the foot – has the effect of calming down a rajasic Vishuddha Chakra, which manifests as obsessive attention to detail and tidiness. Conversely, balancing postures will spur into life a tamasic Prithvi Tattva, which can manifest as an inability to take action or move forwards on a project.

This beautiful posture can be accomplished by even those who are as yet only able to go into the lotus posture with just one leg, as its major requirement is balance.

1 Stand in simple tadasana (see page 40). Take your weight onto one leg and allow your head to align over that heel. Feel yourself growing tall over that leg as it takes more weight. Then bring the other leg into a half lotus, with the foot resting on the upper thigh.

2 Bend down and touch the floor. Let the muscles at the back of your neck release and lengthen. This is extremely important in the balancing process: lengthened muscles at the back of the neck will signal to the body that you are in control of your movement.

3 Bend your supporting leg and simultaneously raise your heel. Allow your body to descend and the full body weight to meet the raised heel at the perineum. Slowly begin to straighten the body and bring the hands up, palms together, over the heart. Allow your body time to organize itself around the point of balance. Hold the posture for one or two breaths, and release. Repeat to the other side.

VṚKṢĀSANA

Tree posture

Again we have a balancing posture that requires us to become deeply rooted while we reach upwards. And, as we release down and extend up, we search for the stillpoint that calms Vishuddha Chakra and brings it into a sattvic state. Vrksasana is a gentle balancing posture in which we are able to focus on that moment when perfect balance is felt in the body, and thus physically experience sattva.

1 Stand in tadasana (see page 40), feet hip distance apart, with your weight releasing down through your body and through the feet, just in front of the ankles. Become aware of your head aligning between the heels of your feet. Feel that as your weight releases down you connect with the earth and become grounded. Feel the simultaneous flow up through your body.

2 Take all of your weight onto one leg. Allow your head to align above that heel and feel yourself become tall over that leg. Raise the other leg and place the sole of the foot on the inner thigh of the supporting leg. Hold your hands, palms together, over the heart.

3 When you feel balanced, reach up with your arms. Maintain the feeling of the weight releasing down, taking care not to allow the sacrum to pull up. It's only as we release down that we can reach up – we are beings earthbound by gravity but with powerful aspirations. These two qualities have to become balanced. Repeat to the other side.

TRIKOṆĀSANA

Three angles posture

This is the 'almost perfect' Akasha Tattva posture. It's a posture of organization and precision – the qualities of Akasha Tattva. If you ever need to activate this tattva, this is the posture to do! As you will see from the completed posture (step 2, opposite), the body forms three angles – the legs form one, the arm extended down and the body form another, and the arm extended upwards and the head and neck form the third. To achieve these three angles we need to focus on each stage of the posture.

POSTURAL INFORMATION

This asana does wonderful things for the neck, shoulders and arms if you can keep the neck lengthened and the shoulders widened as you hold it. Emerging from the cervical vertebrae is a tramline of nerves that supplies the chest and arms, called the brachial plexus. Once you are in the posture, when you turn your head these long nerve fibres are forced to move and become clear of any adhesions within muscles and other tissue – enlivening and reorganizing them. Pain in the neck, shoulders and arms that has no mechanical or physiological source, and is therefore thought to be due to disruptive sensory pathways, is often relieved by this posture.

1 Stand with your feet roughly three feet apart and your arms extended out at shoulder height. Turn the toes of one foot out (towards the side you will be extending down into) so that the feet form a ninety-degree angle. Make sure that the heel of the out-turned foot is in line with the centre of the other foot as this ensures stability through the posture.

Ensure that your hips and shoulders are facing the front, and that the hips aren't tilted to the side.

Don't draw your weight upwards in either your legs or your abdomen. Always remember, when you do standing postures, that you engage proper muscle tone by releasing your weight down – then the natural intelligence of your body, rather than muscle tension, takes up the muscle tone that's needed to keep you upright.

Be careful not to allow your shoulders to lift up around your ears. Let them release and widen – become aware of the point between the shoulder blades from which the arms are extending, and let your hands grow further and further apart.

Stay aware of your breathing.

WATCHPOINT Don't let your hip tilt outwards or forwards, or you will lose the valuable stretch. Ensure the shoulder doesn't drop forwards, and that the upper chest stays open. Don't let your shoulders 'crowd' the neck – let them continue to widen, allowing the back to remain open and supportive of the breath.

2 Allow your whole torso to lengthen and the front of the spine to open. Breathe in, and as you breathe out take your body down to the side, over the out-turned foot. Reach down the leg as far as you can. If you can, place your hand on the floor behind your foot. Once the posture is steady, lengthen the muscles at the back of your neck, turn your head and look up at your upstretched hand. Hold the posture, breathing. Repeat to the other side.

MAHĀ MUDRĀ

The great seal

The word *mudra* means 'to seal'. In this posture, both the top and the bottom of the body are 'sealed', and so the prana is held in an internal flow. In maha mudra, the prana is forced to move between Muladhara Chakra at the perineum and Vishuddha Chakra at the base of the neck. Thus it not only connects our capacity for actualization with our ability for organization, but serves to integrate one with the other.

- Stretch one leg out at a slight angle. Place the heel of the other leg at the perineum. Take hold of the toes of the outstretched leg. This completes the external; what happens internally is of equal importance.
- Simultaneously, do the following: push the perineum down into the ground; as you breathe out, contract the abdominal muscles and draw the abdomen back towards the spine; lengthen the muscles at the back of the neck and draw the chin in and down, and press the tip of the tongue against your teeth.
- Take your attention down to Muladhara Chakra at the perineum and let it flow up sushumna nadi to Vishuddha Chakra.
- Relax the abdomen and breathe in.
- Repeat to the other side.

FURTHER TECHNIQUES

MUDRĀ

The purity and expansive nature of Akasha can only be likened to the sky or to pure consciousness. The power of this chakra is to organize matter from chaos into the order of creation – this requires the consciousness of this vitality to be pure and unblemished. *Chit* is a Sanskrit word not easily translated. It's consciousness of the 'self', beyond the boundary of the skin or the individuality. It's the seer, the witness – and this state of pure witness, in which even the mind is observed, is the requirement of this mudra.

Sit in padmasana (see page 93), resting your hands on your thighs, palms facing upwards. Arrange the fingers of both hands in Chin Mudra (consciousness gesture) by bringing the tip of the index finger down to touch the root of the thumb. Remain in Chin Mudra for as long as you wish.

LIFESTYLE CONSIDERATIONS

Akasha Tattva is the energy of organization, of making order out of chaos. Toxicity can easily put this chakra off balance. Occasional fasts or semi-fasts can help to clear the system of a toxic build-up. These fasts should not just consider food – think of fasts from technology, from companions, from talking, and so on.

- Akasha and Vayu Tattvas together form the Vata constitutional 'dosha' of Ayurveda, and although these chakras are in the throat and chest region of the body, this dosha primarily affects the large intestines. This can make for variable bowel function that easily goes from diarrhoea to constipation. Consider consuming various healthy oils as an essential part of your nutrition.

- An active Akasha Tattva makes for creativity, but if it gets overactive (rajasic, see page 32) this can become restlessness that doesn't settle into creating. Again, add time spent alone in tranquil surroundings to your day. Also think of adding regular massages with heavy oils, such as sesame oil, to your weekly routines.

- Aloe would be a wonderful plant to add both to your massage and also into a drink each day. It cleanses the liver and spleen and promotes balance.

PRĀṆĀYĀMA

The phase of prana in Vishuddha is the inhalation called, simply, 'prana'. All of us breathe all the time. However, the stress of living a modern urban lifestyle dramatically affects and inhibits our breathing. Our bodies breathe following the simple rule of all gases: gas moves naturally from an area of high pressure to an area of low pressure. When we have exhaled, the pressure in our thoracic cavity (where the lungs are situated) and the pressure in the atmosphere are equal. Then, powerful muscles cause the floor of the thoracic cavity (the diaphragm muscle) to descend and the ribs to lift and spread out. As space is thus created in the thoracic cavity, the air pressure in it becomes lower, and gases in the atmosphere – following their rule – flow into the lungs. What we must remember, therefore, is that inhalation, and particularly deep and satisfying inhalation, relies entirely on the freedom of these muscles to move. Tension anywhere in the body can inhibit the movement of these muscles and thus inhibit the free flow of respiration.

EXERCISE

Sit quietly in a chair that supports your back, and tune into your own body to discover its movement as you breathe:

- Place your hands over your abdomen and feel for movement there. As you breathe in, your abdomen should expand outwards under your hands. This is the diaphragm descending and the muscles of the abdomen making way for that descent. If your abdomen doesn't expand noticeably, don't try to force it out – this will only create more tension. Rather, pivot forwards from your hips and place your elbows on your knees. Drop your head forwards and start to focus your breathing into your lower back – the lumbar region. Feel the muscles there expanding out to the side as you breathe in, and coming back down as you breathe out. A few weeks of doing this daily, for about three or four minutes at a time, should correct the problem.
- Check your jaw, throat and shoulders for tension. With each inhalation, visualize your shoulders and back widening as you breathe in. Allow the muscles in the back of your neck to lengthen and release, and, while keeping your lips together, let your teeth part slightly as your jaw relaxes.

MANTRA

'HAM'

VISUALIZATION

Visualize yourself sitting beside a vast lake. It's night and the surface of the lake is broken by a gentle breeze – scattering the image of the full moon high in the sky into fragments across its surface. You can see the outline of the trees around the lake as you sit quietly and peacefully, feeling perfectly safe and secure. In this place nothing can harm you. Gradually allow the ripples on the lake to become calm as the breeze dies down. Now the full moon becomes a perfect reflection in the centre of the still waters. As you watch, a single lotus in bud slowly breaks through the surface in the centre of the reflection of the moon. It moves so slowly and gently that it doesn't create even a ripple. The sky is beginning to change as a silvery predawn light starts to appear and, as you watch, the lotus begins to open sixteen perfectly formed smoky-coloured petals. From its white centre the seed sounds begin to flow out of it with the sacred pranava mantra on either side: Om Ham Om.

Allow yourself to listen to this sound as long as your attention can be held. Feel your whole body responding to this imagery, and each cell of the body reorganizing itself around the experience. Feel that all five bodies – koshas – from the causal, through the intellectual, emotional, vital and physical, are being brought into alignment by the power of this mantra.

Situated behind the heart, this chakra is the focus point of Vayu Tattva – the power of movement. Vayu is more correctly translated as 'wind'. Here we see the full force of the intention as it moves from potential to actual. The dark void begins to let in light as movement is generated. If Akasha Tattva is the germinating seed, then Vayu Tattva is the first snowdrop bursting through the hard ground of winter – forcing its way towards the light.

This is the tattva of all kinetic energy, be it electrical, chemical or pranic. It's quick growth that surges forwards through all obstacles. It is unpredictable – its outcome can only be anticipated. It's random and moves everywhere, moving everything that it touches – like the wind lifting and dropping dry leaves and twigs. Vayu is the gentle breeze that cools and the hurricane that rips through everything – and it's all the states of air or wind between these two.

ANĀHATA CHAKRA

the power of air

PRANIC PHASE

The pranic phase associated with Vayu is *vyana*. Vyana is responsible for the movement that distributes prana throughout the body. So the movement through all the nadis from all the chakras, and the movement between the chakras themselves, is the work of vyana. It's the mighty push the heart gives to the oxygen-filled blood on its journey through the body, and the impulse of the small muscles of the arteries to maintain that movement.

EFFECT ON MIND AND BODY

Vyana causes the impregnated ovum to move from the darkness of the fallopian passage into the grey light of the womb, where it begins the process of differentiating and communicating. This chakra governs the formation and impulse of all the communication systems in the body, particularly that of the nervous system. Generating our sense of touch, it governs our ability to open ourselves to the paradox that our greatest security lies in our vulnerability, in allowing the world to touch us just as we touch the world. Vayu moves us to continue the process of becoming: the cells that form the primitive streak in the embryo, and which become the brain and spinal cord, also form our outermost covering, our skin – forever uniting the inner and the outer.

A tamasic state in this chakra will express itself in increasing alienation. The inner world will become more and more discordant with the external world as we slowly 'lose touch'. Feelings of powerlessness will be experienced, and this will be visible externally, as the shoulders rotate forwards and slump, becoming lifeless. The Anahata Chakra connects to our hands, and the conduits from heart to shoulder to hand become stiff and lose communication with each other.

A rajasic state in this chakra will express itself through impatience. As well as feeling alienated, we will feel misunderstood, have outbursts of temper, lose the capacity to negotiate and insist on always getting our own way.

THIS CHAKRA IN ASCENDANCY

If this chakra has a natural ascendancy in you, you will be a highly motivated person, always able to accomplish projects on your own initiative. You will not shy away from leadership but rather welcome it. Your resourcefulness will be admired by everyone, although you will have to take great care that you don't override other people's wishes too often. You respond positively to pressure and you never hesitate to act on your will. You jealously guard your freedom.

ESSENTIAL VAYU TYPE

The essential Vayu type is the warrior prince or princess. This is the person who rides into battle leading from the front. The natural Vayu type may not be good at forming a team, but they certainly know how to command leadership. They are bold and will ignore their own safety to ensure the safety of others. They are the protectors of the values of the community, and will not think twice about standing up to opposition. Essential Vayu types naturally wield power, and others naturally give it to them.

UṢṬRĀSANA

Camel posture

One of the most challenging things we can do in life is make ourselves vulnerable. As we grow older we become more defensive. We even adopt a posture of protection around the heart. Our shoulders rotate forwards, our chin pushes out to lead the head forwards and slowly we close ourselves around a heart that we are closing down. Too many blows, disappointments, broken promises, shattered dreams. And our posture, defensive and burdened, is witness to the disappointments of our lives as we close in around our heart.

The heart, leaning in from the left, sits in the centre of the chest. Gently enfolded by the soft tissue of the lungs, and protected by the hard bones of the spine at the back and the breastbone in the front, the heart connects and integrates the entire body via arteries, veins and capillaries. Its persistent and regular rhythm sends oxygen and nutrients to every cell of the body, feeds the ever-hungry brain and central nervous system, and collects the body's wastes for disposal. Its sacred beat makes our minds think, our muscles move and our lungs breathe. It's a humble and obliging sovereign – hollow but never empty.

Ushtrasana challenges our defensiveness – opens us, makes us vulnerable and allows us to experience the very deep security that can be found only in our vulnerability and openness. In this posture, the prana of Vayu Tattva is able again to break free of the restrictions we have placed on it.

1 Sit in vajrasana (see page 39), breathing consciously. Come up onto your knees, ensuring the knees are hip distance apart, and release your weight down through the knees and legs into the earth, allowing the spine to flow upwards. Place your hands on the back of your hips and slowly begin to lift the breastbone and allow the hips to move forwards. Draw the shoulder blades down and together as you slowly continue the journey back.

2 When you have gone back as far as you can, reach down towards your heels and, with full control, take your head back – don't let it 'drop' back. Continue to draw the shoulder blades down and together. If the shoulder blades come up and the shoulders draw up, you have gone further than your muscles are able to – release the posture. Once in position, hold it for two or three breaths, breathing into the top of the chest, and then come up slowly and sit back in vajrasana. After you have completed ushtrasana, you should release the lower back by going into shankhasana (see page 89) for a while, and doing some conscious breathing.

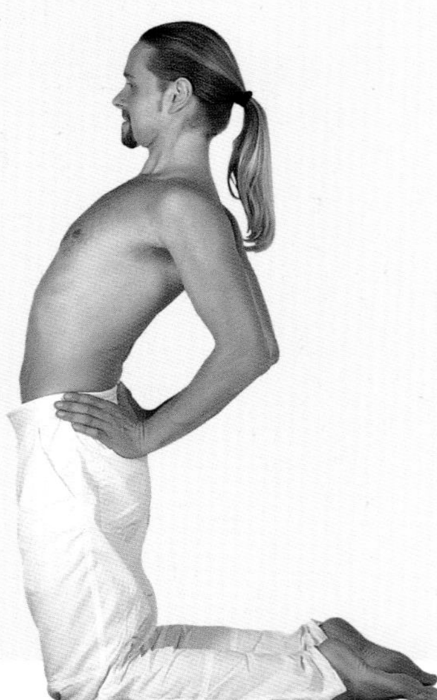

BHUJAÑGĀSANA

Cobra posture

In the previous section, Vishuddha Chakra, you will have tried urdhva bhujangasana – rising cobra. Now, in Anahata Chakra, we reach for a more intense opening of the chest and the heart, and activation of Anahata Chakra. Given that the difficulty for Vayu Tattva is smooth flow of movement, this posture allows this prana to direct its flow rather than scatter.

Before attempting the posture it would be wise to do the preliminary back-opening and backbending stretches from the 'Warming up' section (see pages 23–9), followed by shankhasana (see page 89) to warm up the muscles of the back before taking them into such a powerful movement. You may find that some of the arm-up routines for shalabasana (see page 95) are also useful preliminary exercises for bhujangasana, as they strengthen the back.

ANATOMICAL NOTES

In this posture, the serratus anterior muscle – the support sling for the entire shoulder girdle – is strengthened, offering a more stable and secure ground for the shoulder.

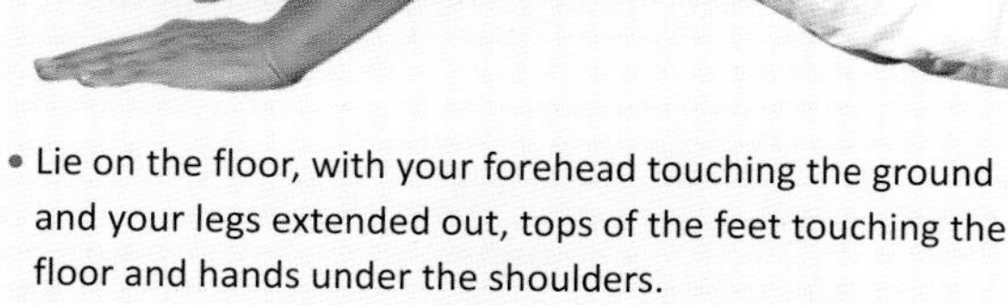

- Lie on the floor, with your forehead touching the ground and your legs extended out, tops of the feet touching the floor and hands under the shoulders.
- The legs don't remain passive in this posture: extend them down from the hips and push the tops of the feet gently down. This might lift the knees off the ground slightly.
- Allow your pubic bone to drop down into the ground and hug the floor – this will stabilize your lower back.
- Draw the shoulder blades down your back.
- Breathe in and raise your head, lifting your body using the power of your back only, and, once raised, breathe out.
- Breathe in and, using the power of your arms, continue to lift your body until you feel you have extended as far as you can.
- Don't completely straighten your arms as the weight may cause the elbows to hyperextend, which destabilizes the very joints transmitting your weight through your arms and hands into the floor.
- Lengthen the muscles at the back of your neck and gaze steadily in front of you with all the magnificent focus of a cobra preparing to strike.
- Feel the front of the spine opening, and become aware of the whole length and bend of the spine.
- Feel the collarbone lengthening as the shoulders continue to widen.
- Feel the chest opening and the prana becoming concentrated and focused in the Anahata region.
- Hold for two or three breaths and then release.

Follow the asana with some conscious breathing in shankhasana.

GOMUKHĀSANA

Cow face posture

The yogis connected the hands with the heart in the pranic body. To them we have both internal and external 'instruments'. Anahata Chakra connects the internal with one of our external instruments – hands. It's a beautiful and simple image to hold in your mind through the day: that what the hands are engaged in directly impacts on the heart, and what the heart feels impacts on the hands. The heart is the great integrator of the body – connecting the cells of the body via the bloodstream. Perhaps it's for this reason that yogis considered it the 'centre of the being'. However, tension in the shoulders prevents this free flow of prana from heart to hands and vice versa. Gomukhasana opens the shoulders and releases these tensions. Throughout the posture, try to maintain an awareness of the connection between Anahata Chakra and the hands, and the shoulders and arms, as the conduit for that connection.

Place your legs out in front of you. Bend one leg and place the heel alongside the opposite buttock. Bend the other leg and place it on top of the leg you have already bent. Tuck the heel in alongside the opposite buttock. Reach up with the arm on the side of the top leg, and reach behind you and up between your shoulder blades with the opposite arm. Drop the hand of the upstretched arm down to meet the hand of the arm reaching behind you. Let the fingers meet, and hold the posture for four to eight breaths, breathing evenly. Repeat to the other side.

ANATOMICAL NOTES

If the shoulder blade on the side of the arm reaching up 'wings' away from the ribs, it indicates tension in the subscapularis muscle. This is a muscle often ignored by bodyworkers, but is one of the major muscles involved in frozen-shoulder syndrome. Ask someone to watch your shoulder blades for 'winging' and, if it occurs, release the stretch and use a strap to make the connection between the hands. In gomukhasana, the serratus anterior muscle that was strengthened during bhujangasana (see page 55) is gently stretched and opened.

CAUTION

If this posture forces your head forwards, release the arms slightly and use a strap to achieve contact between your hands. Don't let the head be forced forwards, shortening the muscles at the back of the neck, as this transmits tension down through the shoulders, so losing the benefits of the posture.

AÑJANEYĀSANA

Hanuman was one of the greatest heroes of Indian mythology. His virtues and heroism are extolled in texts like the *Ramayana of Tulsidas* and the *Ramayana of Valmiki*. He was a fearless warrior and humble devotee of Vishnu, whom he worshipped as Prince Rama. His father was Vayu (Lord of the Wind) and his mother was the charming Anjani. This asana honours her.

In this posture we again stretch wide open the serratus anterior muscle that supports the entire shoulder girdle and lift the ribs – the sturdy basket in which the heart nestles. Again the body has a chance to release tensions that have inhibited the free flow of prana from heart to hands and vice versa. By integrating the shoulders with a hip-opening exercise, as in this asana, we also connect the heart to the lower part of the body, giving the prana the opportunity to flow downwards and upwards. Remember: we never seek to isolate the prana in one chakra, but rather to stabilize and direct its flow.

1 Come to a kneeling position on the floor and swing one leg forwards so that the thigh is parallel to the ground and the knee and ankle joint are in line. Take the other leg back to lie flat on the ground behind you. Let your hands remain on the floor for a few minutes while you let your ribs sink on to the thigh and release down into the ground, allowing the hips to open and the thigh of the leg extended back to release and lengthen.

2 Slowly straighten your body and breathe in deeply, raising your hands over your head and reaching up with your arms. Let the entire basket of the ribs lift up and away from the hips as the pelvis and legs yield to gravity and sink down. Join the palms, and keep extending and reaching upwards with the top half of your body while the lower half sinks down – gently grounding that runaway Vayu prana. Repeat to the other side.

WATCHPOINT Ensure that your front knee remains reaching forwards directly in front of you, and doesn't drop to the inside or to the outside and thus destabilize the hip joint and the flow of prana.

VASIṢṬHĀSANA

After the young Prince Rama had taken his first journey out of the palace walls to see the country he was to govern, he returned fitful and depressed. When the sage Vasishtha visited the palace, Rama's father asked him to find out what was troubling his son. Rama tells Vasishtha that his heart is heavy because of all the suffering he witnessed beyond the palace walls. The human condition seems to be one filled with sorrow. In a spectacular teaching that came to be known as the *Yoga Vasishtha*, the sage answers all of Rama's questions and restores his equanimity.

Like Prince Rama, our hearts become heavy too. This powerful prana of Vayu Tattva can become dampened by sorrows. Sometimes we look at our place in the world and we feel overwhelmed and inadequate. We use vasishthasana to remind ourselves of the strength we have when we work with the 'I' that is beyond the ego – the self that is limitless and always adequate.

1 Begin in dandasana, with the body in a perfectly straight line, the toes tucked in and the hands assisting the feet in supporting the weight of the body (see page 62).

2 Turn one foot so that the outside of the foot rests entirely against the floor, while you continue to give yourself balance with your hands. Rest the other foot and leg on the ones underneath. Look down the length of your body – don't let the hips drop towards the floor.

3 Slowly raise the arm that's not supporting your weight overhead, and bring the arms into a straight line.

4 Turn your head and look up at your upstretched hand. Hold the posture for a few breaths. If your arm begins to shake, drop the lower leg and place the knee on the floor. Repeat to the other side.

PARIVṚTTA JĀNUŚIRṢĀSANA

Rotating head to knee posture

Along with allowing the vitality of Anahata to feel support, we also need to open it and integrate it again with the shoulders, hands, hips and legs. By rotating the body, the deep, small paraspinal muscles are strengthened and stretched. The posture thus locates and releases deep inner tension in the thoracic area around Anahata Chakra, which might be containing its dynamic vitality.

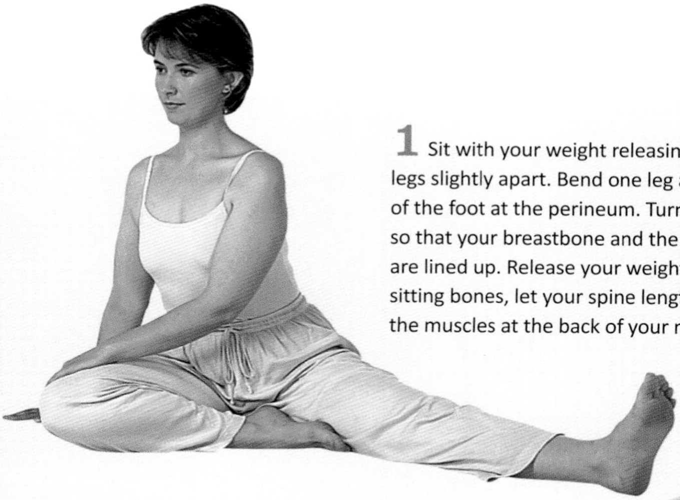

1 Sit with your weight releasing down and your legs slightly apart. Bend one leg and place the heel of the foot at the perineum. Turn your whole torso so that your breastbone and the thigh of the bent leg are lined up. Release your weight down through your sitting bones, let your spine lengthen and flow up and the muscles at the back of your neck lengthen.

2 Place your corresponding hand on the straightened leg and slowly begin to release down. Ensure that you don't drop the shoulder forwards and thus rotate the body forwards. Let your head release. Breathe in and slowly raise your arm, reaching up into the space above you.

3 Bring your other arm over, reaching towards the toes of the outstretched leg. Feel the ribs opening and the intercostals being stretched – they are primary muscles of breathing, and this posture directly challenges any poor breathing habits we have acquired as well as tension in the intercostals. Keep releasing down as you reach over. Breathe into the open and extended ribs. Hold for five to ten breaths, and repeat to the other side.

WATCHPOINT Don't let your shoulder and arm drop in front of your face – you will lose the stretch of this posture.

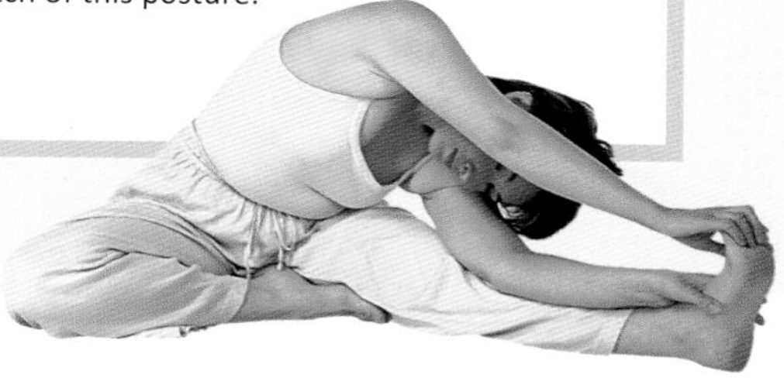

UTTĀNĀSANA

Forward stretch posture

In the next few postures, we open the back of the thorax, just as we have been opening the front in previous asanas. The shoulders are still being extended and opened. Uttanasana is a forward stretch that draws the heart towards the thighs and encloses the front of the body, while the back is exposed and opened. It acts in the same way as ushtrasana to engage the vitality of Anahata Chakra, but opens the back of the body instead of the front.

ANATOMICAL NOTES

The cells of the nervous system, neurones, are found within the spinal canal. Extensions called 'processes' extend from the neurones; and 'axons' are the processes that connect the spine and the skeletal muscles. The nerve cells that control your big toes, for example, are found in the spinal column but their axons extend from the spine right down to the muscles of your toes. In an extreme forward flexion like uttanasana, the spinal canal is lengthened by as much as three inches – the extension occurring mostly in the cervical (neck) and lumbar (lower back) regions. This allows the axons to move and clear away adhesions and blockages, stimulating the entire nervous system.

1 Stand in tadasana (see page 40) with your feet hip distance apart and the weight releasing down through your body, with your head aligning between your heels.

3 Take hold of your big toes or rest your hands on the floor in front of you. Draw your head towards your knees and hold the posture, maintaining your breathing. Focus your attention on the heart being drawn into the thighs and the spine behind the heart opening. Let the sitting bones rise up towards the ceiling and the sacrum pivot upwards. Hold for between five and ten breaths, and then release.

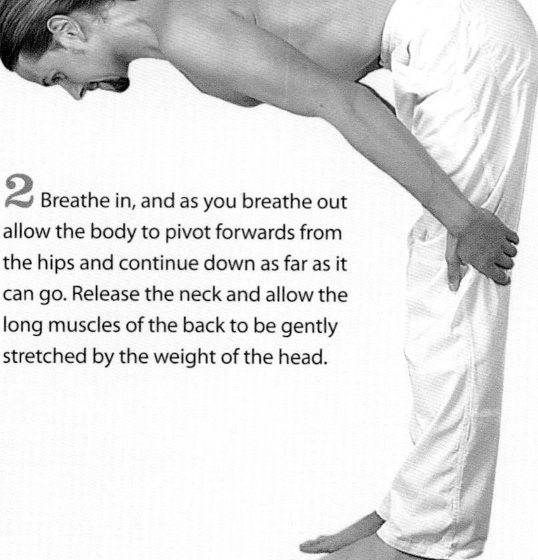

2 Breathe in, and as you breathe out allow the body to pivot forwards from the hips and continue down as far as it can go. Release the neck and allow the long muscles of the back to be gently stretched by the weight of the head.

HALĀSANA

Plough posture

The most extreme opening for both Vishuddha and Anahata Chakras comes from this dynamic posture. Again the heart is drawn in and protected in the front, and opened and exposed at the back. Just as a plough is used to break up ground so that new seeds may be planted, so halasana performs a similar function for us.

Repetitive and protective patterns that cause us to rotate our shoulders forwards and shorten the muscles at the front of the neck are challenged by postures that open the front of the body. In these postures, where we open and stretch the back, we are 'ploughing' the field to implant new and exciting patterns of behaviour, which are more creative and meet the lives we are now living.

1 Lie flat on the floor, with the back of your head on the ground and the muscles at the back of the neck lengthening. Go into sarvangasana, supporting your back (see pages 42–3). If a shoulderstand creates too powerful a stretch on your neck in this posture, place a folded towel under your shoulders.

2 When your breathing is steady and your face, neck and shoulders have released into the posture, drop one leg down behind your head. If this is too difficult, you can place a chair behind your head and drop your feet onto that.

CAUTION
If you feel any discomfort, release the posture immediately.

3 If your breath remains steady, drop the other leg down, keeping your feet slightly apart to avoid tension. Again, become aware of your head and your spine lining up directly between your heels. Drop your hands and place your palms down. Hold the posture for a few even breaths. Think of the ribs as a basket holding the lungs, with the heart nestled between them. Remember: Anahata Chakra is the place of the 'unstruck sound'. Visualize this chakra, just behind the heart, gently opening and Vayu Tattva streaming from it into your heart and from your heart through your entire being.

VARIATION Once you feel fully confident in this stretch, you can increase the work by parting your legs and taking your hands up towards your feet.

DANDĀSANA

Staff stretch

After halasana, relax in shavasana for a few seconds (see below) and then do a gentle but powerful dandasana. This creates a feeling of support for all the movement that has been happening through the previous postures and also reminds the serratus anterior to support the shoulder girdle.

Danda is the staff that the yogis used as they travelled – never staying in one place or getting attached to anything. Dandasana, staff posture, gives the vitality of the heart that same support. As we move through life, the heart contacts many people and places and it loves them – that is its nature. When it becomes stuck anywhere, it has gone against its nature. Dandasana reminds us that the support we need is there as we move onwards – always ready to embrace and love the new with the old.

1 Move onto all fours, knees hip distance apart and heels of the hands under the shoulders. Take a step back with one leg and then the other, and support the weight of the body on the hands and on the toes, which are tucked under. Ensure that the body doesn't drop down or the buttocks push up. Hold the posture, breathing steadily. When you are ready to release, gently drop your knees on to the floor and go into shankhasana (see page 89) for a few minutes.

ŚAVĀSANA

Corpse stretch

If yoga contained only one of its forward bends, one of its backbends and the corpse posture, it would still be a highly formidable body and vitalitywork system. In shavasana we can truly get in touch with the deepest level of Anahata Chakra. Vayu Tattva, like Agni and Akasha, will always have a tendency to become rajasic, while Apas (water) and Prithvi (earth) have a tendency towards tamas. In shavasana, as we release the whole of the body into the ground and allow the full effect of gravity to flow through us, we restrain and retrain Vayu Tattva. Then it's possible to enter into a deep communication with Anahata Chakra – to become aware of this place of silence that carries the tapering flame of our individual consciousness in its windless silence.

- Lie on your back, with your legs slightly apart and your arms slightly away from your body, palms facing upwards. Neither the legs nor the arms need to hold tension in this posture.
- Allow the breath to flow deeply into the body, and with each exhalation feel your weight flowing down into the earth.
- Become aware of the contact you have with the ground at the back of the head, the arms and the hands, the shoulder blades, the back of the hips, buttocks, thighs, calves and heels, and with each exhalation allow the weight to flow down through these specific points of contact into the earth.
- Allow your shoulders to just drop back, and feel the collarbone lengthening.
- Slowly become aware of the breath as the only movement of the body. Feel the abdomen rise up and away from the spine as you breathe in and then sink back down towards the spine as you breathe out. After a few breaths, move your awareness to your chest and feel it move up and out as you breathe

in and sink back down as you breathe out. Next, become aware of the ribs and feel them expanding as you breathe in and coming back down as you breathe out.

- Now begin to fix your whole attention on the outbreath. Follow its course – keep following its flow to that stillpoint between breaths.
- Become totally absorbed in that stillpoint between the exhalation and the next inhalation. When the breath ceases to move, the mind ceases to move. Simply watch. Watch for the very first movement that gives rise to the next breath. Watch closely enough and you will become aware of the impulse to breathe that arises before even the first movement. Allow yourself to enquire and probe that impulse. What is it that 'breathes' you?

SUPPORTED ŚAVĀSANA

One of the kindest things you can do for your spine is give it support in shavasana. Roll up a rug or towel and place it along the whole length of your spine. Also roll up a small hand towel and place it across the rug at the back of the neck (see above). In this position every segment of the spine feels support – including the cervical vertebrae at the back of the neck, which are rarely supported yet provide all the support for the head, and which act as a link between the head and the heart. Once you are in position, observe your breathing as above.

ANANTĀSANA

Infinity posture

Once you have entered into the silence of Anahata Chakra and contacted its profound peace, it's time to distribute that bliss and peace throughout the body. In an easy move, you can roll over from shavasana into the infinity posture, and as you go into the posture feel the vitality of Anahata Chakra, which has taken on the qualities of Vayu – movement and dynamism – flow through the entire network of nadis in the body. The physical body, arranged around the individual consciousness, is not the seat of our infinite nature. As we extend outwards into external space, we need to remain aware of our inner space and seek out that self within the heart that belongs to infinity.

1 Roll over from shavasana onto your side. Ensure that your legs are extended straight down. Support your head on your hand and bend the top leg, bringing the knee towards your head. Then take hold of your big toe, breathe in and, as you breathe out, straighten and lengthen your leg. Hold the posture for a few conscious breaths. Make sure that you aren't allowing the leg extended on the floor to bend at the knee. Release and repeat to the other side.

WATCHPOINT If you are unable to straighten your leg holding your toe, use a strap as an aid. Never try to force yourself into a position – remember that your body will place its own natural limitations on you.

BANDHA TRAYA
Lock of three

Bandha traya is similar to maha bandha but even more powerful in effect. The prana is forced into the upper body and then, on release, cascades down through the rest of the body like water that has been held back under pressure. Swami Venkatesananda says the following about bandha traya:

> *This bandha ties up the network of nadis and thus prevents the downward flow of nectar from its source above the palate. Thus the nectar is saved from being consumed by the gastric fire.*
>
> *When the yogi practises these three bandhas together – the Mulabandha (contracting the rectum and perineum), Jalandhara Bandha (contracting the neck) and Uddiyana Bandha (contracting the abdomen) – prana and apana unite and enter into the Sushumna Nadi. Then the prana is no longer agitated. It becomes steady. This is Bandha Traya.*
>
> YOGA, SWAMI VENKATESANANDA

EASY POSTURE

Sit on a folded towel. First, bend the most mobile knee, placing the foot against the inner thigh of the opposite leg. Bend the other knee, placing the foot in front of your other foot (put cushions under your knees to support them, if necessary).

1 Sit in padmasana (see page 93) or sukhasana (easy posture) if your knees and hips aren't mobile enough for padmasana (see above right).

2 Lengthen the muscles at the back of the neck and, making a powerful forwards flexion, bring your chin onto your chest.

3 Breathe in and push the breath down. At the same time, draw up the pelvic floor muscles towards the navel. Hold this posture for as long as you are able to hold your breath, and then release by raising your chin and breathing out.

FURTHER TECHNIQUES

MUDRĀ

The heart is the centre of being – the integrator of the entire body. Anahata Chakra, behind the heart, is the place of silence from which the first movement in the vitality arises. It governs the sense of touch, and thus rules the hands. In this mudra, we experience the sensation of hand touching hand, and observe the movement of the breath. This is the initiating vitality, the impulse that moves towards visible life.

Sit in padmasana (see page 93) and bring your hands together. This is known as Anjali Mudra. Focus the awareness of Anahata Chakra and allow a feeling of humility to fill the heart – a humility at the immensity of this vast, pulsating movement that is life. Before you release the mudra, feel that you are offering a greeting to life, and feel it welcoming you in return.

LIFESTYLE CONSIDERATIONS

Vayu Tattva, like the wind, is movement. Balance in both Vayu and Akasha Tattvas gives us movement that's creative and meaningful. When unbalanced, these two tattvas – which give us the Ayurvedic dosha known as Vata – can lead to restlessness and a sense of listlessness.

- Vayu Tattva is governed by Anahata Chakra, the chakra in the spine corresponding to the heart plexus of nerves. The ancient rishis of India said this place is the seat of self, the heart of (our) matter! Maintaining self-awareness that leads neither to self-obsession nor to negative self-judgement, is the task of this vitality. A single flame is the central imagery of this chakra – and like that single flame, we need to keep our self-awareness alight in the winds of life.
- As with Vayu, make oil massages part of your routine, adding to whatever base oil you use, including essential oils such as rose and lotus. The heart chakra's tendency is to take us outwards towards others and we must honour this movement. However, again as with Vayu, you need to make time for yourself to be on your own, with your own thoughts and contemplations. Think of making a space in your home that's your own 'sacred space' and spend time there.
- Consider beginning your day with a cup of hibiscus flower tea instead of coffee (which can throw Vayu into a rajasic state). The hibiscus flower imparts a gentle contemplative energy that doesn't put us to sleep but makes us aware of the more subtle energies around and within ourselves.

PRĀṆĀYĀMA

Prana here enters the phase of vyana – distribution. All forms of exercise will increase and improve distribution of the blood throughout the body. Yoga *vinyasa* (postures done in a sequence) are particularly useful for improving blood flow. The pranayama exercise that exerts the most powerful influence on the nervous system, which is influenced by Vayu Tattva, is nadishodhana pranayama – the nadi-purifying breath. It involves alternate-nostril breathing and has a particularly powerful impact on ida and pingala nadis, balancing the forces of contraction and expansion.

NĀḌĪŚODHANA PRĀṆĀYĀMA

Take up a comfortable seated posture, close your eyes and tune in to your breath:

- Become aware just of the left nostril – feel the air entering and leaving through the left nostril. Then begin to feel the air in the left side of your throat and chest. Become aware of the left side of your head, face, ear and neck as you breathe in and as you breathe out. Let your awareness begin to incorporate the whole of the left side of your body: shoulder, arm, left side of the chest, abdomen and pelvis, and leg and foot. Keep your awareness there, and then switch your attention to the right side of your body, and do the same body-awareness exercise on the right. Note any difference in how the right and left sides of the body 'feel'.
- Now you are ready for nadishodhana pranayama. Bring your right hand up and block the right nostril with your thumb (don't 'push' your nose), and breathe in through the left nostril. Then, with the right ring finger, block the left nostril and breathe out through the right. Now block both nostrils with thumb and ring finger and hold the breath out for a few seconds, then breathe in through the right and out through the left. Repeat this for about nine rounds.
- Finish by again becoming aware of the left and right sides of your body as you breathe normally, noting any differences brought about by the exercise.

MANTRA

'YAM'

VISUALIZATION

Again, place yourself beside your tranquil lake. It's still predawn but the sky is brighter now, even though the sun isn't visible. The breeze has built up once more. You can feel it against your skin and see it rippling the surface of the lake and moving the leaves on the trees. The birds are beginning to awaken and you can hear their soft chatter humming through the trees around you. Then you notice a lotus in bud burst up through the surface of the lake – it doesn't rise gently, like the previous one, but comes up with an urgency. Just as quickly, it opens its bright gold petals to the sound of a loud clap of thunder and then, as soon as the petals are opened, everything becomes silent – breeze, birds and water, everything waits with bated breath. Slowly, from the luminous centre of this golden lotus its bija mantra begins to flow: Om Yam Om. As it does, the breeze resumes and the birds continue their soft chatter – all sounds merging with the sound of Om Yam Om. Feel the movement in your own body as your vitality responds to this awakening. Become aware of your breath and your heartbeat. Feel every cell in your body awakening to a new day and accelerating its use and production of energy.

Situated behind the navel, Manipura Chakra is the focus point of Agni Tattva – the power of fire. Here the prana has the power of transformation. The potential of Akasha and the movement of Vayu take form through the transforming power of Agni. Here the prana is the giver of light – the child is born into light from the grey of the womb and differentiates from the mother. The ahamkara, the idea-of-I, is born and we see ourselves as beings separate from other beings. Parts of the body have fully organized themselves into separate tissues – lungs, heart, liver, muscle and so on. The germinating seed, having burst through the ground, now flowers.

MAṆIPŪRA CHAKRA

the power of fire

PRANIC PHASE

The stage of prana influential in this chakra is samana, the prana responsible for transforming food into nourishment. Once the oxygen has been sent on its way through the blood vessels via vyana prana, the tissues and cells of the body must take up the oxygen and, through the power of their own alchemy, transform it into energy and carbon dioxide by means of metabolic process. Samana prana is responsible for transforming food into nourishment, and information into ideas.

EFFECT ON MIND AND BODY

This chakra governs our sense of sight – by its light we see. But this sight must also be our inner vision and we must learn to let it guide us as surely as the sight of our physical eyes guides us. We can often tell the state of the vitality of this chakra by the sparkle in a person's eye – or lack of it. This chakra can imbue the whole body with sight if we let it. The hand and foot will touch and 'see' as surely as the eye. The power of fire and its gift of sight also mean being able to see that which is 'other' and which threatens – so it's the 'sight' of the immune system.

A tamasic state in this chakra will lead to a lowered immune response along with a loss of energy. Our sense of self-worth will become diminished as our vision – internal and external – is impaired. Digestion and absorption of nourishment become sluggish and poor, and this is reflected in the mind as we become less and less able to discern truth from falsehood. A rajasic state in this chakra will often lead to an aberrant immune response – as in allergic reactions. The digestion will be overstimulated, and this will result in excess digestive juices, causing acidity, heartburn and ulcers. It might also cause diabetes and hypoglycaemia. More than any other chakra, Manipura is susceptible to highs and lows, creating great peaks and troughs in energy levels.

THIS CHAKRA IN ASCENDANCY

If you are someone in whom this chakra has ascendancy, you will have that wonderful ability to transform every situation you encounter. People coming into contact with you will feel that they have been touched by something special and feel changed by the meeting. You will allow people to see the extraordinary in what they usually see as mundane. As a salesperson, you will be unequalled, as anything you take into your hands to sell will immediately be imbued with the qualities of a magic wand. You will be persuasive and have an outstanding gift for speaking and expression. You will never be happy just standing still and will continually want to move on to the next thing.

ESSENTIAL AGNI TYPE

The essential Agni type is the healer or the performer. Their touch will bring a magic that people respond to instantly. As a performer or actor on stage or screen, this type will naturally attract attention – they will make us believe their performance. As a healer, their perceptive sight will heighten their intuitive abilities and allow them to see beyond the clinical data – an X-ray, or the results of the blood test, perhaps. Time and again they will go directly to the problem as if it were obvious. And their remarkable sales skills will allow them to convey the healing process to the patient in ways that can be easily followed and understood. They will always make the patient feel that the two of them are working together towards health, and their patients will never feel that remedies have been imposed upon them.

PAŚCIMOTTĀNĀSANA

Back extension posture

This is one of the most demanding postures of yoga and one of the foremost postures for activating Agni Tattva, and thereby eliminating accumulated toxins from our system, boosting our immune system and improving our circulation. As you bend forwards, organs like the stomach, liver, spleen and intestines are gently squeezed and massaged, and then as you release the posture they are bathed in a flow of blood.

Here, the long muscles of the back and the back of the legs are stretched. Indeed, the word *paschimottanasana* can be broken up as follows: *paschima* – 'behind' – and *uttana* – 'extension'. That which is behind is the experience we have already undergone, and many of our past tensions are locked in these long muscles. Do this posture honouring that past, and allow the muscles time to stretch and release those long-held tensions rather than forcing them and driving the tensions inwards.

CAUTION

If you are in the first trimester of pregnancy, avoid this posture as it puts stress on the womb. After the first trimester, it can be practised gently, but keep the legs slightly apart so as to avoid any stress on the womb.

- With your legs stretched out in front of you, release your weight down through your sitting bones. Become aware of your breathing.
- Release your shoulders and let them widen as you release the muscles in the back of your neck and allow them to lengthen.
- For a deep but gentle stretch, draw the top thigh muscles up slightly towards the hips. Feel the backs of the legs being stretched and flattened onto the floor.
- Inhale and, as you exhale, lengthen the front of your spine and lean forwards, pivoting the crest of the hips.
- Continue this downward stretch until you have reached the Asana Awareness Zone. If you are able, take hold of your feet – classically it's the big toe that's grasped, but you can also take hold of the outer edges of each foot.
- Allow the weight of your head to drop forwards and the muscles at the back of your neck to lengthen further.

WATCHPOINT If the muscles of your neck, shoulders and jaw become tense in this posture, place your arms on a stool, rest your forehead on your arms and remain there. Breathe deep into the lower back, feeling the muscles there expand and contract with the breath.

WATCHPOINT People often struggle in this posture. Pulling yourself forwards using your shoulders and arms won't get you into the posture any quicker. In fact, the tension you create will cascade through the body and further tighten the muscles you are trying to release.

NAṬARĀJĀSANA II

Inside the body, a perpetual dance is being performed by nutrients and chemicals necessary to maintain life. We call this dance metabolism, and its purpose is to build up and break down. It builds larger structures from smaller ones – for example, binding amino acids to make proteins, and binding proteins and lipids to create cell membranes. In this stage we call it anabolism. In its breaking-down phase we call it catabolism, and in this phase, larger structures, like food, are broken down to become viable nutrition and energy. Natarajasana I, which we do to encourage the creative Akashic phase, belongs to the anabolic process of the body and mind. Natarajasana II, however, belongs in the Agni, or catabolic, phase.

The great god Shiva, giver of the wisdom of yoga, takes on both postures to maintain life. Nataraj is the name given to Shiva when he's engaged in this dance.

1 Stand in tadasana (see page 40). Allow your weight to release down through your body, legs and feet, and feel your spine flowing upwards as the muscles of your neck lengthen and your shoulders release and widen. Feel your head aligning between your heels.

2 Take all your weight onto one foot and become aware of your head aligning above that heel. Feel yourself becoming tall over that leg, then bend the opposite knee and take hold of the ankle. Breathe in gently, and as you breathe out draw your leg back and raise the opposite arm. Hold your thigh lift parallel to the ground – even if you feel you can raise it further. Holding this position without letting your body drop forwards will gently open the hip of the raised leg and strengthen the opposite one.

ARDHA BADDHA PADMĀSANA

Half-bound lotus posture

While Akasha (space), Vayu (air) and Agni (fire) tattvas are more prone to becoming rajasic, and Apas (water) and Prithvi (earth) are more prone to becoming tamasic, Agni can on occasion lose vitality and become just an ember. This is possibly because modern living requires such breakneck speed. The half-bound lotus posture acts on the muscles surrounding Manipura Chakra and opens up the whole area – allowing the vitality to flow through and enliven Manipura, while also enclosing the vitality and keeping the flow within the body.

1 Sit on your mat with your legs stretched out in front of you. Let your weight release down through your sitting bones and feel your whole spine lengthening. Bend one knee and place the foot on the opposite thigh.

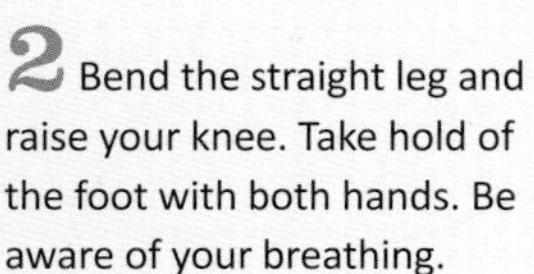

2 Bend the straight leg and raise your knee. Take hold of the foot with both hands. Be aware of your breathing.

3 Breathe in, and as you breathe out gently rock back to balance on your sitting bones and slowly straighten your leg. (If you are unable to straighten your leg, use a strap.) Give your body time to find its point of balance. Take care to continue breathing evenly. Allow your jaw and shoulders to relax and let the shoulder blades flow downwards, releasing any tension that has crept into the upper body. Hold for about five or six breaths – breathing into the lower back – and then slowly release and repeat to the opposite side.

JĀNUŚIRṢĀSANA

Head to knee posture

You can continue the work of the half-bound lotus posture with janusirshasana. This continues the process of opening the back around the lumbar and lower thoracic area. Fritz Smith MD says in his book *Inner Bridges* (see 'Further reading' on page 141), 'A person cannot not react.' It's a wonderful and affirming thing to see this statement written down. We react to everything – and it's often the 'gut' reaction that's the most significant. This reaction is frequently transferred to the back, and the muscles around the area of the lower thoracic vertebrae and lumbar area become tightened and hypertonic. Postures like janusirshasana open and release this area if we do them without struggle – without reaction – and release the body into them.

The important thing to remain aware of while in this posture is your breathing. Direct the breath to your back and feel the movement of the back as you breathe. As well as the lengthening they are experiencing, the muscles of the lower back will expand outwards as you breathe in and contract as you breathe out. Keep your attention on this movement, allowing each breath to take the back into greater and greater release.

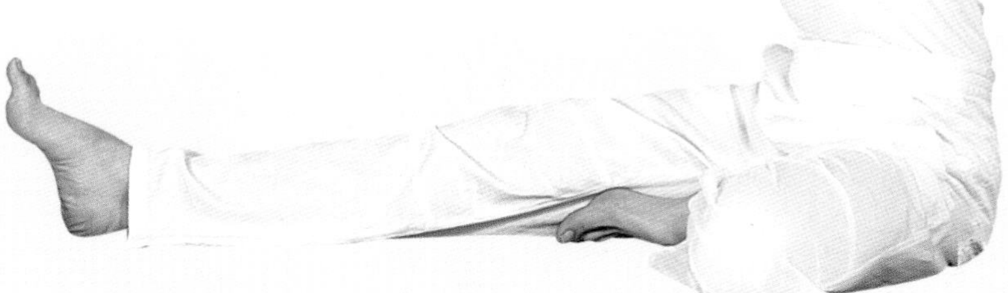

1 Having completed the half-bound lotus (see opposite), remain on the mat with your legs extended out in front of you. Bend one knee and place the heel of the foot into the groin. Breathe in and raise your arms overhead. Breathe out, releasing your weight down through your body and down into the earth through the sitting bones. Feel the spine flowing upwards.

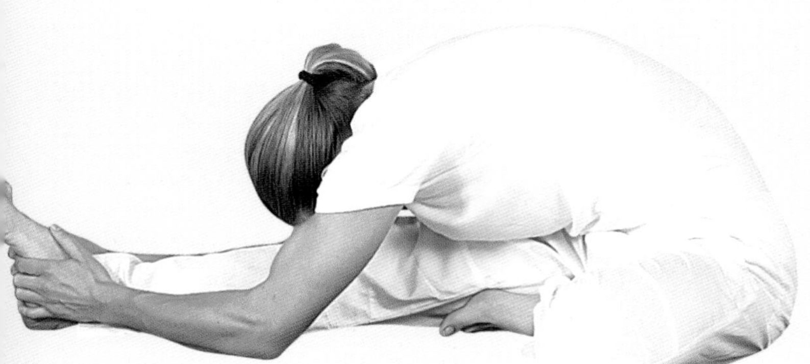

2 Breathe in, and as you breathe out pivot forward from the hips, extending your arms and body down your outstretched leg. Release your body down into the thigh of the extended leg but don't force this – pivot forwards as far as you can and then release all effort and let your body yield to gravity. Hold the posture, breathing into the back for about five or six breaths – feel your back opening and releasing its tension. Repeat to the other side.

CHAKRĀSANA

Chakra posture

Having opened the back of the spine and released tensions around the powerful postural muscles through the stretches earlier in this section, we can now begin to open the front of the spine to continue to act on Agni Tattva. It's this 'fire within' that drives us to make contact with the world outside. It imbues us with a desire to connect with our fellow creatures on this planet, to communicate with them and to know them. However, the prana needs occasional withdrawal into Apas (water) and Prithvi (earth) to be replenished. When that doesn't happen, it can become exhausted. If this occurs, do some of the postures from the 'Earth' and 'Water' sections and follow them with some powerful 'Fire' activators like these.

In this asana, the spine is bent in the opposite direction from its usual curves. This often serves to awaken the spine. Important structures in the soft tissue of the body are constantly in a 'report-back' mode to the central nervous system, telling the brain about the condition and activities of the body. If there's an overload on any particular muscle or group of muscles, our brain instructs those muscles to go into an adaptation to accommodate the stress. This adaptation is individual to each person (or animal) and may appear as muscles becoming fibrosed (laying down fibrous tissue) or even as the spine going into a slight rotation. When this happens, the tissue around the area will generally be tense, contracted and tired. These powerful backbends reawaken the body to new and alternative ways of adapting to the stress, and also change the old patterns of behaviour in our muscles.

The renowned osteopath Irvin Korr said the following of the spinal cord:

> *The spinal cord is the keyboard on which the brain plays when it calls for activity or for change in activity. But each 'key' in the console sounds not an individual 'tone', such as the contraction of a particular group of muscle fibres, but a whole melody of activity, even a 'symphony of motion'. The brain 'thinks' in terms of whole motions, not individual muscles.*
>
> MODERN NEUROMUSCULAR TECHNIQUES, LEON CHAITOW

In chakrasana, our attention is called to this activity of the body, as powerful postural muscles are called into action to achieve the final posture.

Before you attempt chakrasana, you may find it useful to attempt the posture using the support of a chair, to get the feel of supporting your body with your hands (see below).

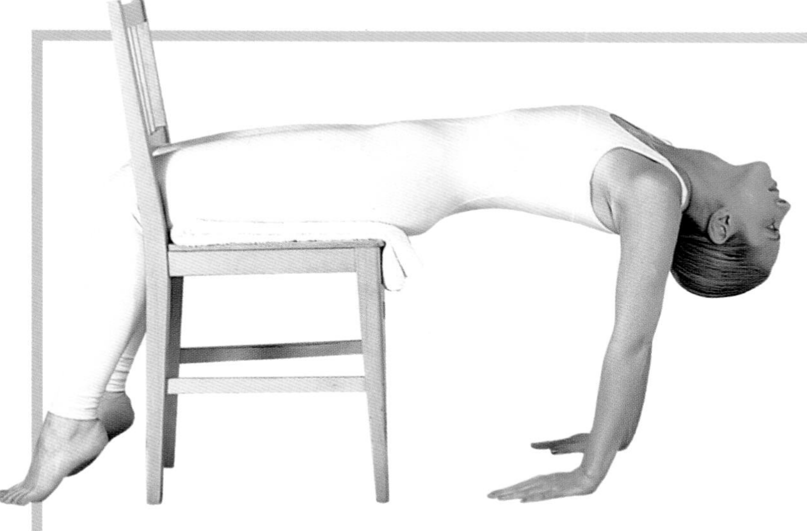

PREPARATORY EXERCISE Sit on a suitable chair, facing backwards, with your legs through the opening at the back. Ensure that your buttocks are on the seat of the chair. Reach down first with one hand and then with the other and place your hands firmly on the floor. 'Walk' your hands so that they are under the shoulders and hold this posture, breathing gently. To release, bring one hand up before the other, taking hold of the chair to help bring yourself up. This can also be done with the help of a partner assisting you in coming down and in returning to an upright position.

Lie on the floor with your knees bent and your feet flat on on the floor, close to your buttocks, and your hands on the floor, just above your shoulders (fingers pointing down towards your body). Breathe and push up through your legs and arms to achieve lift. Allow your head to gently yield to gravity. Hold the posture for just two or three breaths, feeling the powerful work of the muscles of the arms and shoulders, back and legs to hold you in this posture. Release slowly, and either bend your knees and hug your legs into your chest, or go into shankhasana (see page 89) and observe your breathing.

CAUTION

People with back pain or fused vertebrae should approach this posture with caution and spend some time on achieving gentle setubandhasana lifts (see below) before attempting this pose. People with high blood pressure should avoid both postures. Neither of these postures should be done during pregnancy.

SETUBANDHĀSANA
Bridge lock posture

In this posture, we strengthen the back muscles as they lift us up against gravity.

- Lie on the floor, with your knees bent and your feet flat on the floor, hip distance apart. Place your hands on the floor, palms down, or take hold of your ankles (use a strap if you are unable to reach).
- Breathe in and lift your buttocks and back off the floor.
- Breathe out, and as you breathe in raise your buttocks further, creating a powerful stretch through the front of the spine.
- Hold the posture for three breaths, feeling the muscles that are contracting powerfully to keep you in this position.
- Remain aware of your shoulders and particularly your collarbone, allowing it to lengthen and the front of the chest to open.
- Become aware of the stretch to the back of the neck.
- To release, slowly lower your body onto the floor and either bend your knees and hug them into your chest or go into shankhasana (see page 89) and watch your breathing for a while.

VĪRABHADRĀSANA II

Warrior II posture

We now encounter the god Shiva in his fearful aspect as a warrior, fixed on battle. The mythology around virabhadrasana centres on a sacrifice being held by the gods, presided over by Daksa, who is one of the Adityas (sovereign principles). Shiva is insulted when he's not invited and his consort, Uma, is killed. Shiva takes on his warrior role to destroy those attending the sacrifice and appears before them as the terrible warrior Virabhadra.

Such mythologies all carry powerful messages for the way we should live our lives. This one reminds us that we do nothing for ourselves alone. When we 'forget' to work from our divine nature and seek to exclude it from our lives, we send into the flames that consort of the divine – awareness. When we remember our own true and divine nature, we have to revive the awareness through discipline and sharp focus. Virabhadrasana II offers us the opportunity to evoke these qualities.

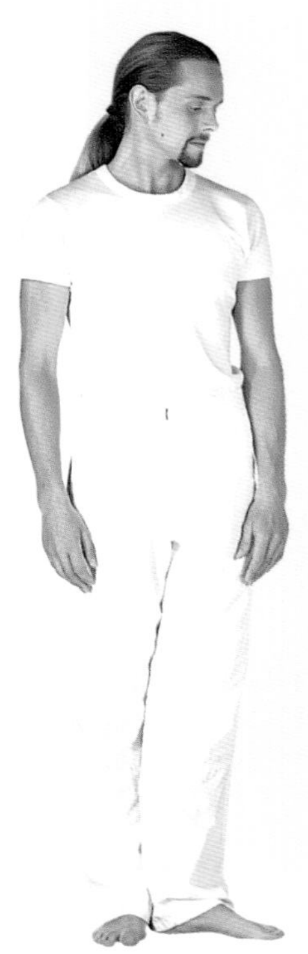

1 Stand towards the back of your mat, with one foot pointing out to the side at right angles, towards the other end of the mat. You are going to take a large step forwards with that foot, so begin by focusing on the point of the mat where you want to place your foot.

2 Breathe in, and as you breathe out take a step forwards, placing your foot roughly four feet away, still keeping it pointing out to the side. Make sure that this foot is aligned with your back foot. The toes of the back foot should still be facing to the front, as should your hips and body.

DHANURĀSANA

Archer's bow posture

Having drawn our courage from the virabhadrasana, we take our bodies into the archer's bow posture – further increasing our attention and focus and thus awakening and balancing Agni Tattva.

Like many backbends, this posture acts powerfully on the psoas muscle – the muscle responsible for initiating the action of the legs to make them walk. We come, then, to another aspect of Manipura Chakra: its influence on the legs. Just as Anahata is connected to the hands, Manipura is connected to the legs and feet. We need to keep this connection free of tensions and blockages in order for the prana to flow freely and for us to be able to 'see' our way ahead and walk our particular path.

PREPARATORY EXERCISE Because this posture acts on the group of muscles on the front of the thigh, known as the quadriceps, it's important to stretch them before attempting the posture. Lie flat on your front, with your head turned to one side and your arms by your side. Bend one leg back and take hold of the ankle. Gently draw the heel down towards your buttock. Hold for a few breaths, giving the muscle time to release its tension and reorganize itself around the stretch. Release, and repeat to the other side.

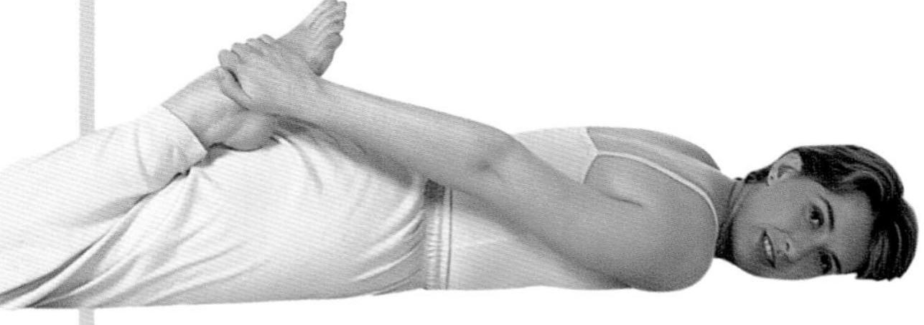

3 Breathe in, and as you breathe out bring your arms up to shoulder height, allowing your shoulders to release and widen. Turn your head to gaze at the fingertips of the hand extended over the front foot.

4 As you breathe out, bend your front knee, yielding down to gravity. Ensure that it doesn't reach over the foot – the ankle, leg and knee should form a straight line, and the thigh should be parallel to the floor. Hold for five breaths, release and repeat to the other side. Follow with shavasana (see page 62).

1 After stretching, remain lying on your front. Place your chin on the floor and bend your legs back towards your buttocks. Take hold of your ankles with both hands. Breathe in, lifting your head, and then breathe out.

2 As you inhale, raise your body and thighs. Be careful not to let your shoulders crunch up around your ears. Keep the back of your neck lengthened by looking straight ahead rather than looking upwards.

ŚIRṢA AÑGUŚṬHĀNA YOGĀSANA

Head to ankle yoga posture

One of the ways in which we lose contact with our vitality is by isolating certain parts of the body as they become stressed. We are born with a body that's fully integrated, in which every part is aware of every other part. Sustained stress – either physical or emotional – causes the body to undergo adaptive processes that often isolate one part of the body from another. The entire 'gut' area is one where many of us hold and store the stress we are otherwise unable to respond to through the day. The major part of restoring the flow of prana through Agni Tattva is reintegration. In this dynamic posture, Anahata Chakra is balanced and integrated with the flow of prana within sushumna nadi from the head to the feet.

1 Stand towards the back of the mat with one foot pointing out to the side at right angles, ready to step forwards down the length of the mat.

2 Breathe in, and as you breathe out step forwards, keeping your foot pointing out to the side and in alignment with the back foot. Keep the back foot pointing to the front.

3 Breathe in, and as you breathe out slowly pivot forwards, taking your head down towards your ankle and reaching upwards with the interlocked hands. Ensure that there's no tension in the muscles of the back of the neck in this final posture, but release the head and allow it to gently lengthen these muscles.

BACK VIEW Interlock your fingers behind your back. Breathe in, and as you breathe out slowly begin to bend the front knee and yield down to gravity, ensuring that the knee aligns over the ankle and that the thigh is parallel to the ground.

HARI-HARĀSANA

Posture of Hari and Hara

Here we encounter Shiva in the form of Hara. The famous epic poem, the *Mahabharata*, declares, '*Sarva bhuta hara*' – 'Hara is he who sweeps away all things'. This is Shiva in his full power of destruction and devastation. However, in this asana it's tempered by the presence of Hari – another name for Vishnu, the great preserver and protector. Each occupies one half of the body and adopts this posture, signifying both devastation and preservation. Part of the work of Agni Tattva is to destroy that which is no longer necessary in our lives. Old emotions, regrets and longings have to be swept away to allow for new experiences. Cells have to die in order for others to live and take our shape. Agni Tattva must also recognize what is to be preserved – it must have the 'in-sight' to protect that which is of value within us. In this posture, we honour both these aspects of Agni Tattva and bring them into harmony and balance.

1 Come onto your knees and step forwards with one foot, placing it firmly on the ground as in anjaneyasana (see page 57). Allowing your back knee to release the weight, gently release down, ensuring that the front knee doesn't extend over the ankle. As you breathe out, reach around and bend your knee to take hold of your ankle.

2 Breathe in, and as you breathe out reach upwards with your opposite arm. Keep yielding down to gravity, allowing the entire pelvic floor area to open and release.

WATCHPOINT Don't force yourself into this posture. If you are unable to reach your ankle, use a strap instead.

SIṀHĀSANA
Lion's posture

It's almost impossible to go through an entire day without encountering situations or people that will engender feelings of irritation or frustration – or even anger. We are not always able to dispose of these emotions outwardly and instead dispose of them inwardly, swallowing back any outburst we may otherwise have made. The place of storage becomes the stomach, where these emotions – while perfectly natural to the human condition – become toxic when left unchecked.

The entire abdominal area can be the casket in which we retain stores of our rage and fear – all those emotions that have been left unexpressed. Here we come into contact with our instinctive self, and for many of us that can be frightening. Tension here is reflected in the throat – releasing one area will begin the release in the other. This powerful breathing technique allows for belly, throat and jaw to undergo a dramatic release – provided you can get into it and really 'roar' that breath out!

This posture allows us to use the breath to access these emotions and consciously expel them – sweep them away – thus embodying Shiva.

- Sit in easy posture (see page 65) or in vajrasana (see page 39). Lean forwards; if you are in easy posture, place your palms on your knees, and if you are in vajrasana (as here), place your palms on the floor in front of you, fingers pointing backwards. (I prefer the latter posture as it opens and stimulates the powerful heart meridian that runs down the inside of the arms.)
- Become aware of any feelings of frustration, irritation or anger that you are storing in your stomach.
- Breathe in and allow the abdomen to expand fully with this inhalation.
- Let your breath connect with these emotions that you are aware of.
- Then, with a mighty roar like a lion, throw your tongue out as you breathe out the emotions the breath has gathered.
- Repeat this roar four or five times, with the same consciousness.

VIPARĪTA KARAṆĪ MUDRĀ

Viparit means 'standing in reverse' and *karani* means 'the practice of'. The posture looks very similar to the shoulderstand, but it's the internal practice that turns this into a powerful anti-ageing action that prevents the powerful Agni Tattva from overwhelming the life-giving, organizational prana of Akasha Tattva. Usually prana enters sushumna nadi at the crown of the head and then flows down through the five major chakras that extend from the throat to the perineum. On its way down, as it passes through the chakras that house the panchatattva, the prana becomes charged with their particular characteristics. The tattva in the throat – Akasha – is the creative or building tattva, while that of the navel is the breaking-down tattva. Both of these are vital for the functioning of the body. However, in their search for enlightenment, the yogis prized longevity and sought to maintain the prana in the throat in order to slow down the ageing and decaying process of the body.

This highly powerful posture appears in the *Hatha Yoga Pradipika* manual, which says the following:

There is a wonderful way
By which the nectar is prevented
From being consumed by the sun ...

Hold the navel above the throat
Thus the sun is above and the moon below
This is called Viparit Karani –
The reversing process
When given by the guru's instruction
It will yield results.

The practice of Viparit Karani strengthens the digestion
Therefore the practitioner should ensure the
availability of food.
If one takes too little food
The heat produced by the sun will destroy the system.
Begin slowly –
For only a few breaths and slowly increase.

This practice should be done daily
Gradually increasing the time it is held.
After some time the practitioner will see
The signs of ageing begin to diminish.
Becoming accomplished at this posture
Means one can overcome even the god of death.

HATHA YOGA PRADIPIKA, CHAPTER 3, VERSES 78–81

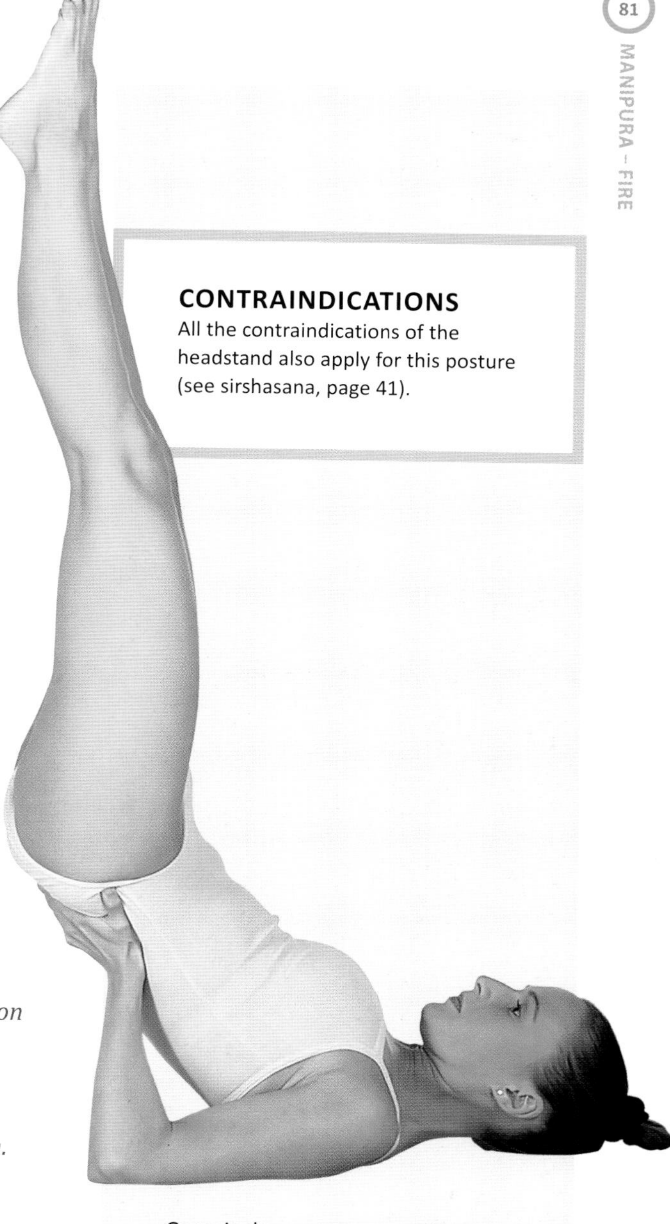

CONTRAINDICATIONS

All the contraindications of the headstand also apply for this posture (see sirshasana, page 41).

Go up in the same manner as if you were going to do a shoulderstand, but don't reach high up with the legs. Get your legs and arms into an angle, as shown above. Once in the posture, practise mulabandha (see page 113) to turn the asana into a mudra and achieve the full benefits.

FURTHER TECHNIQUES

MUDRĀ

Fire stands between the unmanifest and the manifest. It has form and yet its form is constantly changing. It's here, in the light of the flame, that the ahamkara (idea-of-I) comes into being. This is the crossroads at which we can choose the path outwards, that leads to the world, or the path inwards, that leads to grace. Be aware of the charged moment and observe the changes in the entire body–mind complex.

Sit in padmasana (see page 93) and reach up with one hand, opening the palm to heaven. Reach down with the other hand, opening the palm and pointing it towards earth. With this gesture, we are giving and receiving prana in equal measure – a perfect pivot between heaven and earth.

LIFESTYLE CONSIDERATIONS

Agni (fire) Tattva and Apas (water) Tattva together form the Ayurvedic constitutional pitta or the fire dosha. Obviously, this has to do with digestion and our digestive fires. However, it would be a mistake to think this is confined to what happens in our stomachs: we take in information through the senses – and buddhi (awareness) and mind (manas) must make sense of it, must 'digest' it for it to become knowledge. All this is the function of the Agni Tattva governed by Maṇipura Chakra.

- Adding a number of vinyasas, such as surya namaskara (see page 117), to your daily exercise and movement routine will help to keep the flame of this chakra alive and well. And if you are prone to inflammation, consider avoiding or reducing sugars and adding an essential oil, such as sandalwood, to a regular massage oil or to your bath.
- Agni Tattva, like any fire, can easily blaze out of control or damp down to an ember. The perfect herb for this chakra is ginger. Ginger is known in Ayurveda as *vishvabhesaj* or 'the universal medicine'. It can calm or stimulate Agni Tattva, responding perfectly to what the chakra needs. A hot morning drink with a small amount of freshly grated ginger would beautifully balance this chakra. If you feel your Agni Tattva is a little overactive, you could add dates to your diet as they increase water and earth tattvas, helping ground us and damp down the fire.

PRĀṆĀYĀMA

The phase of prana in Manipura Chakra is samana – the prana of transformation. This is the body's ability to transform what it has procured from the environment in the form of food or breath, which it has distributed throughout the system. Oxygen must be transformed in the cells – via the alchemy of metabolism – into carbon dioxide and energy. Food must be converted into sugar that can be stored. There are a number of wonderful pranayama exercises to stimulate these processes. One that is a challenge to learn (fire is stimulated by challenge) but is extremely powerful is called *agnisara*: 'fanning the flame'.

AGNISĀRA

Stand with your feet a little more than hip distance apart and place your hands on your thighs. Allow the arms to take the weight of the body so that the abdominal muscles may relax completely. Focus on your breath:

- Focus on breathing in and out, engaging the muscles of the abdomen more than usual. Breathe in (always through the nostrils), allowing the abdomen to expand; breathe out and engage the abdominal muscles, drawing the abdomen back towards the spine as you exhale completely.
- Don't pause between breaths. As soon as you have exhaled, release the abdominal muscles and allow for a smooth in-breath.
- Don't allow tension to creep into your jaw, shoulders or neck. Keep the muscles at the back of the neck lengthened throughout.
- Agnisara is the smooth flow of a complete exhalation followed by a complete inhalation, with full engagement of the abdominal muscles, and without any pauses between, seeking to bring the inhalation into equal length with the exhalation.
- Complete about five breaths to start with. Slowly increase this to about eighteen in one practice.

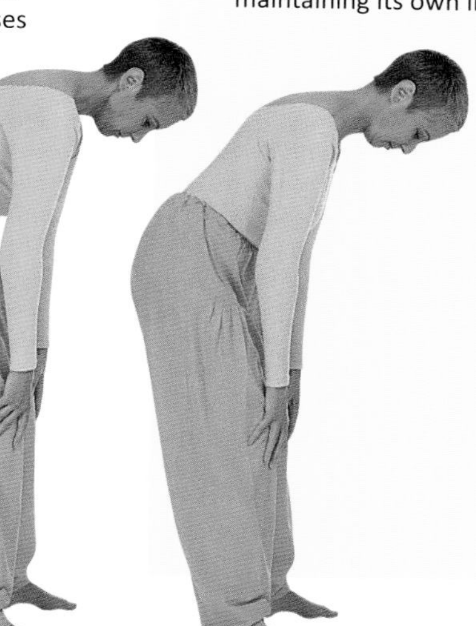

CAUTION
If you are pregnant, suffer from high blood pressure, cardiovascular disease or hiatus hernia, don't attempt this breathing exercise.

MANTRA

'RAM'

VISUALIZATION

You are still at your lake – your place of tranquillity and peace. Nothing enters here that you haven't invited or created. The sun has risen high in the sky, and you can feel its gentle warmth on your face and shoulders. Birds fly overhead, and you can hear the scurry of squirrels and deer among the trees. Rest your hands on the earth and feel how cool the grass is despite the warmth of the day. Look out across the lake at the two lotus plants already growing there – the smoky-purple-petalled lotus alongside a golden-petalled lotus. Now see, rising in their midst, a lotus bud with petals as bright as a yellow canary. As it opens, you see in its centre a blazing fire that forms a triangle, with its apex pointing downwards. Its seed mantra hums out – joining the sounds all round it: Om Ram Om. Feel your body becoming energized and your cells humming with the activity of transformation they were created for. Visualize this fire in every cell of your body – always busy breaking down sugars in the presence of oxygen and producing the energy you will use to fulfil your purpose. As you watch, see how, in the midst of the bright sunlight, all things meet while retaining their integrity. Trees and plants mingle and blend, and clouds scurry across the sky, collide and bond. Feel your entire system taking on this vitality – each part aware of and knowing every other part, even while maintaining its own integrity.

Situated at the base of the spine, Svadhisthana Chakra is the focus point of Apas Tattva – the power of water. Water is the source of plenty, of abundance of every kind. This is matter seething with creative energy and vitality. It's the pregnant water of the womb, which bathes the child as it develops and then helps it break free, bursting forth to open the uterus for birth. Now the individual, born of water, must begin the process of learning to be human – of reaching his or her full potential. We have gone from germination to pushing through the dark earth to flowering – in this chakra, the flower must be pollinated in order to reproduce itself.

SVĀDHIṢṬHĀNA CHAKRA

the power of water

PRANIC PHASE

The prana associated with this chakra is *apana*, the out-breath – the release of that which the body no longer needs to nourish itself. Prana, vyana and apana are complementary. Prana is indicated by the term *ha*, meaning an 'active, solar force', while apana is indicated by the term *tha*, meaning an 'inactive, lunar force'. Bringing these together gives us *hatha*, indicating the uniting of these two forces – which is the power of hatha yoga. Between prana and apana are vyana and samana, which draw them both together.

EFFECT ON MIND AND BODY

This chakra is the seat of will and resolution. It's the power to move around or overcome obstacles in the process of returning to our own true nature. We come from the darkness of Akasha – the void – through the grey light of Vayu into the full blaze of sunlight in Agni, and now we begin to return to the darkness of the waters. In this darkness, the objects of the world begin to lose their differentiation and we again move towards becoming one – but not quite yet. This is the energy of the river descending towards the ocean and nourishing life along the way, without that being its purpose. However, it's also the water that ascends as vapour and returns to earth to irrigate fields and valleys. Here we see life being served even while the goal of oneness is the sole purpose.

Svadhisthana Chakra governs our sense of taste, which allows us to discern what is good and what we can accept into ourselves from the outside. It's this sense that will give us the ability to make the adaptations – even at micro-levels – that will continue the inexorable process of evolution. This is the chakra that houses our most potent creative powers and deepest ancestral memories – the chakra of dreams and fantasies out of which genius is born. When this chakra becomes tamasic, we lose fluidity and become rigid in body and mind. Our creativity dries up and our inner landscape becomes barren. We quickly lose focus and lose the natural act of giving freely – this gives rise to fear and anxiety that, in turn, forces us into reclusiveness and inactivity. This chakra in a rajasic state might lead us deeper and deeper into fantasy that's never brought into the light of the world.

THIS CHAKRA IN ASCENDANCY

If you are a person in whom this chakra is in ascendancy, you will find that the external world is never as fulfilling and enriching to you as your internal world. The work you are engaged in will matter less than the internal environment in which you are ceaselessly creating, questioning and probing. You will be able to conduct your life in a seemingly normal fashion, but beneath the surface you are working out the answers to eternal questions. You will have the ability to build an exceptionally rich fantasy life, and out of this will come inspirations that you will be willing to give away to others. Service to others comes naturally and easily to you – giving what you have seems the most natural thing in the world, and you never weigh up how much you have given or what you are owed in return.

ESSENTIAL APAS TYPE

The Apas type is the philosopher or cave-dwelling yogi. This is the person fascinated by what lies behind the world perceived through the senses. They probe for the truth, which often leads them to become solitary and reclusive. The cave provides more than enough space, as they are really living in an internal world in which they delve deeper and deeper into the mysteries of life. While they may live an ordinary life, their rich inner life will often lead them to strange places and situations after middle age.

NIRĀLAMBANA PAŚCIMOTTĀNĀSANA

Unsupported back extension posture

During this asana the weight of the body pivots on the sitting bones and the base of the spine at Svadhisthana Chakra. As we draw the legs towards us, opening and lengthening the muscles at the back of the legs, more of our weight flows down into this focus point. It brings to mind the nature of the movement of water – always to flow down, following the line of least resistance.

If unchecked within us, this flow of energy can create a tamasic state. But we can also harness and use this flow to draw our attention inwards. Central to yoga is a teaching that litters all the great texts: that of *shreyas* and *preyas*. All our activities fall into one of these two categories. *The Katha Upanishad* says:

There are two paths, O Nachiketas,
One path leads outward and the other inward.
You can walk the way outward that leads to pleasure
Or the way inward that leads to grace.
Of these two it is the path of grace,
Though concealed, that leads to the Self.

THE KATHA UPANISHAD, CHAPTER 2, VERSE 1

All our yoga practices must be put towards assisting us to see the inward path – and then to journeying down this path. Activating and taking the prana to Svadhisthana Chakra will aid us in this endeavour.

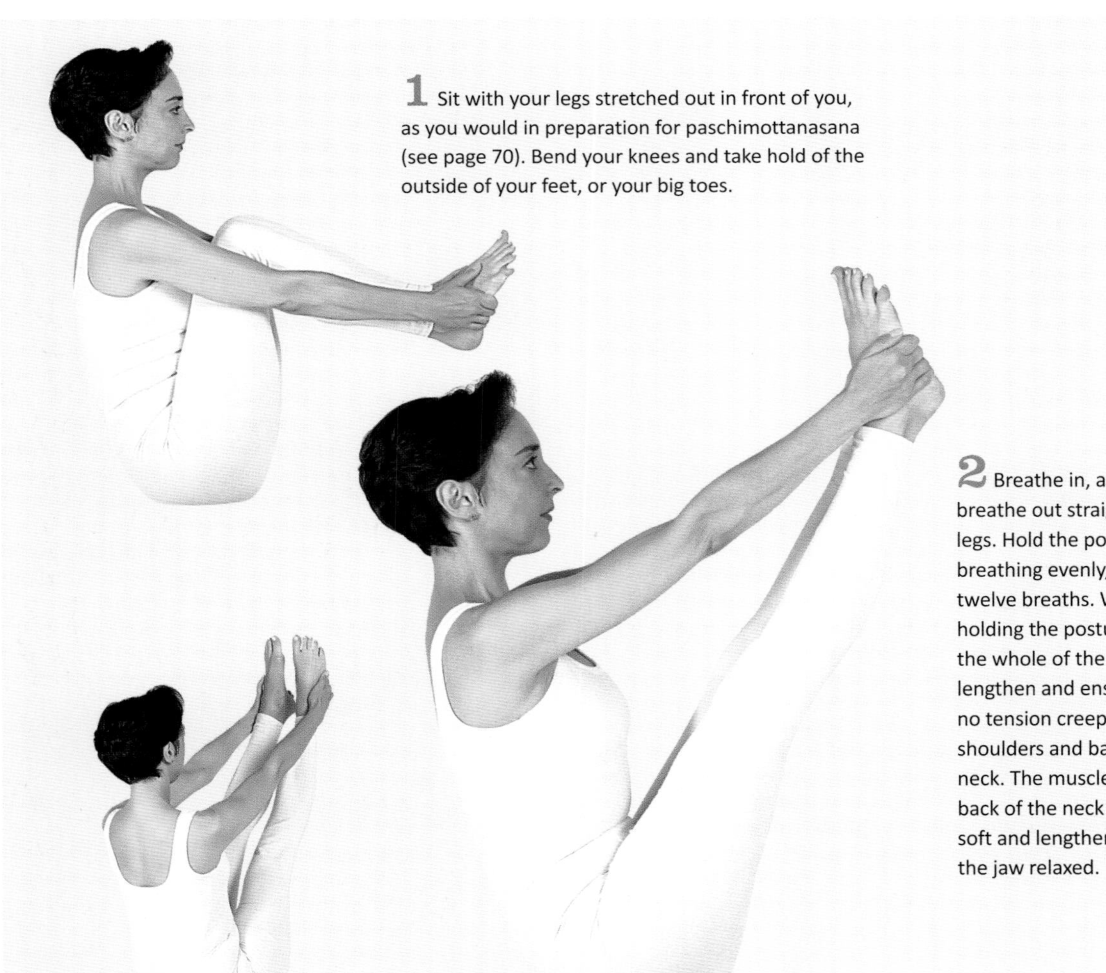

1 Sit with your legs stretched out in front of you, as you would in preparation for paschimottanasana (see page 70). Bend your knees and take hold of the outside of your feet, or your big toes.

2 Breathe in, and as you breathe out straighten your legs. Hold the posture, breathing evenly, for about twelve breaths. While holding the posture, allow the whole of the spine to lengthen and ensure that no tension creeps into the shoulders and back of the neck. The muscles at the back of the neck should be soft and lengthened, and the jaw relaxed.

1 Begin sitting down with legs outstretched. Pick up and hug one leg to your body, as if you were cradling a baby. Gently rock it from side to side.

2 The rocking action begins to warm the hip joint and thereby thin the synovial fluid, enabling its movement within the cartilage of the joint.

3 Next, supporting the ankle with one hand and the knee with the other, trace large circles with the knee. Feel the range of motion in the hip joint.

4 Keeping the raised leg supported with the left hand, place your right hand palm down on the floor.

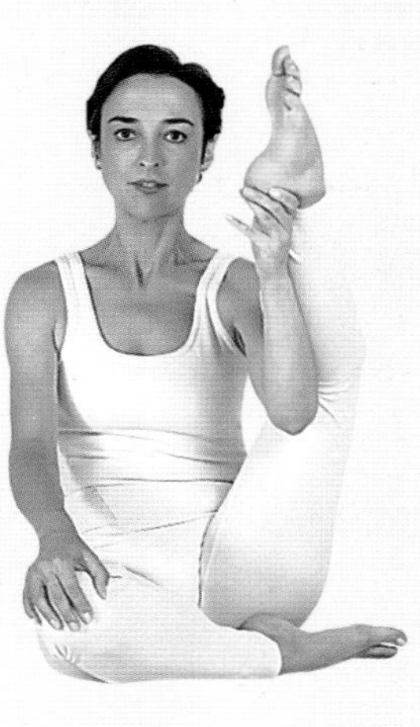

6 Bend your knee and draw the leg back gently towards your chest. Hold this for three breaths. Then place your right hand on the floor, hold your foot with your left hand again and straighten, as in step 5.

7 Now bend your left knee again and, taking hold of the foot with both hands, draw the foot slowly towards your chin. Stop within your own zone of asana and hold for three breaths.

8 Bend your right knee and place the foot alongside the left buttock. With your left hand support the left heel, draw the knee back and raise the heel as high as you can. Hold for three breaths, allowing the Om mantra to vibrate through you. Repeat to the other side.

ARDHA CHANDRĀSANA

Half moon posture

The moon has a strong influence on water; this posture calms a rajasic Svadhisthana Chakra, which makes us withdraw internally. Remember: we seek balance and harmony between inner and outer.

First try the posture with support. Then, when you are ready to reach down and up simultaneously, you will reintegrate parts that feel separate from the whole. Here, we recognize that the body is a whole, made of parts that are all aware of each other.

PREPARATORY EXERCISE Before trying the posture, become aware of the relationship between your leg, hip, shoulder and arm. Go onto your knees, stretch your left leg out and back, and place your right hand on the floor. Extend the left arm up, moving it to explore the space. Feel through the sensations in your body. Repeat to the other side, noting the differences and which side is easiest.

1 First, use a chair for support. Begin with your 'easier' side. Stand in tadasana (see page 40) and turn the toes of the foot nearest the chair outwards. Drop your body down to the side until it's parallel to the floor, placing your hand on the seat of the chair. Simultaneously, raise your arm and extend it up while you raise the other leg, holding it parallel to the floor. Hold for six to nine breaths, feeling the sensations of alignment as they occur in the body. Repeat to the other side.

2 Once you are comfortable with the chair as a support, use a box or blocks that are lower than the chair, and repeat step 1.

WATCHPOINT You are not ready for this final posture if your body and top shoulder are dropping forwards. Use a support until the body is released and strengthened enough to hold a beautiful and straight half moon line.

3 Once you feel steady in step 2, repeat the exercise without support. Your body will now drop lower than parallel to the floor as you extend down with the one arm, finding the support it seeks on the ground, and reach upwards with the other. Ensure that the raised leg is held parallel to the floor.

PADMĀSANA

Lotus posture

This is probably the best-known of all yoga postures. It's certainly one of the most ancient asanas and is one that finds mention in the *Hatha Yoga Pradipika*:

> *This lotus posture is the destroyer of all diseases.*
> *But it is attained only by the wise of the earth.*
>
> HATHA YOGA PRADIPIA, CHAPTER 1, VERSE 47

After the activity of ardha chandrasana, we go into quiet repose and lock the prana within through this powerful posture.

- Extend both legs out in front of you, bend the left leg and place the foot on the right thigh.
- Bend the right leg, placing the foot on the left thigh.
- Place your hands either resting in your lap, one hand on top of the other with the palms facing upwards, or resting on your thighs, forming either Chin Mudra (see page 50) or Jnana Mudra (see page 114). Rest in this posture, observing the breath, for as long as is comfortable.

CAUTION

In most of us, the knee joint isn't capable of the extreme flexion required by this asana. Forcing your knees into it will damage cartilage and ligaments within the joint (both slow healers!). Practise with one leg at a time, allowing the knee to drop as the muscles of the thigh release. Only attempt this posture when comfortable in vajrasana (see page 39).

PRASĀRITA PĀDOTTĀNĀSANA

Legs spread extension posture

In this enlivening stretch we reach down and curl into ourselves – opening the back and allowing that which is behind us to come to the forefront of consciousness. Water is the holder of our memories and dreams – even those of our deep ancestral past. Simultaneously, as we pivot the base of the spine and the sitting bones skywards, Svadhisthana Chakra reaches up and claims the flow of prana. This asana has a wonderfully balancing and rehydrating effect on Apas Tattva.

CONTRAINDICATIONS

If you suffer from glaucoma or a detached retina, remember to avoid all inversion postures. If you have high blood pressure, seek advice from a medical practitioner first.

1 Stand on your mat (or a non-slip surface) with your feet as wide apart as is comfortable for you. Ensure that the legs are not so wide apart that the muscles are unable to hold the posture and the legs start sliding apart – this can cause injury to muscles in the groin. Begin by releasing the weight down through the body and legs, allowing the outer edges of your feet to release down into the mat.

2 Pivot forwards from the hips and place your hands firmly on the floor, if possible with the elbows slightly bent to avoid tension in the shoulders. Lengthen and release the muscles at the back of the neck. Become aware of the base of the spine and the sitting bones beginning to pivot skywards – gently allow the sitting bones to provide the lift.

3 Using about ten per cent of your strength, draw your thigh muscles up towards the hip and continue to allow the sitting bones to pivot upwards as you step back with your hands and drop your head down on to the floor. Your hands should now be between your feet.

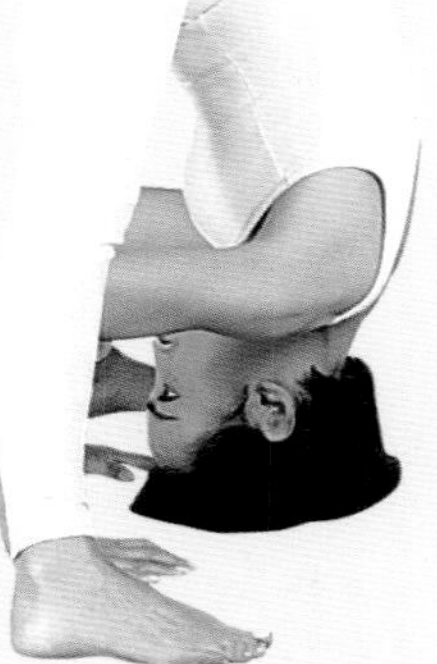

FRONT VIEW Hold the posture while remaining aware of your breathing and how it changes in this inversion as the abdomen crowds the thorax (chest). Keep your shoulders relaxed and open and turn your attention to Svadhisthana Chakra. Feel the prana entering there and flowing down the spine towards the crown of the head. Feel your legs remaining proud, dynamic supports for this movement of vitality. If you are unable to reach the ground with your head, lay a folded blanket down and rest the crown of your head on that instead.

ŚALABHĀSANA

Locust posture

This posture requires the entire area around Svadhisthana Chakra to be engaged: the muscles of the lower back, abdomen and legs have to work with each other to achieve lift in the lower body. Like the locust, whose body size makes 'lift-off' the most difficult part of flight to achieve, this asana requires the vitality to become keenly focused on the areas that will be providing strength, while the upper part provides support and balance.

Before you attempt this powerful posture, spend a couple of months strengthening the muscles of the back with the three exercises below.

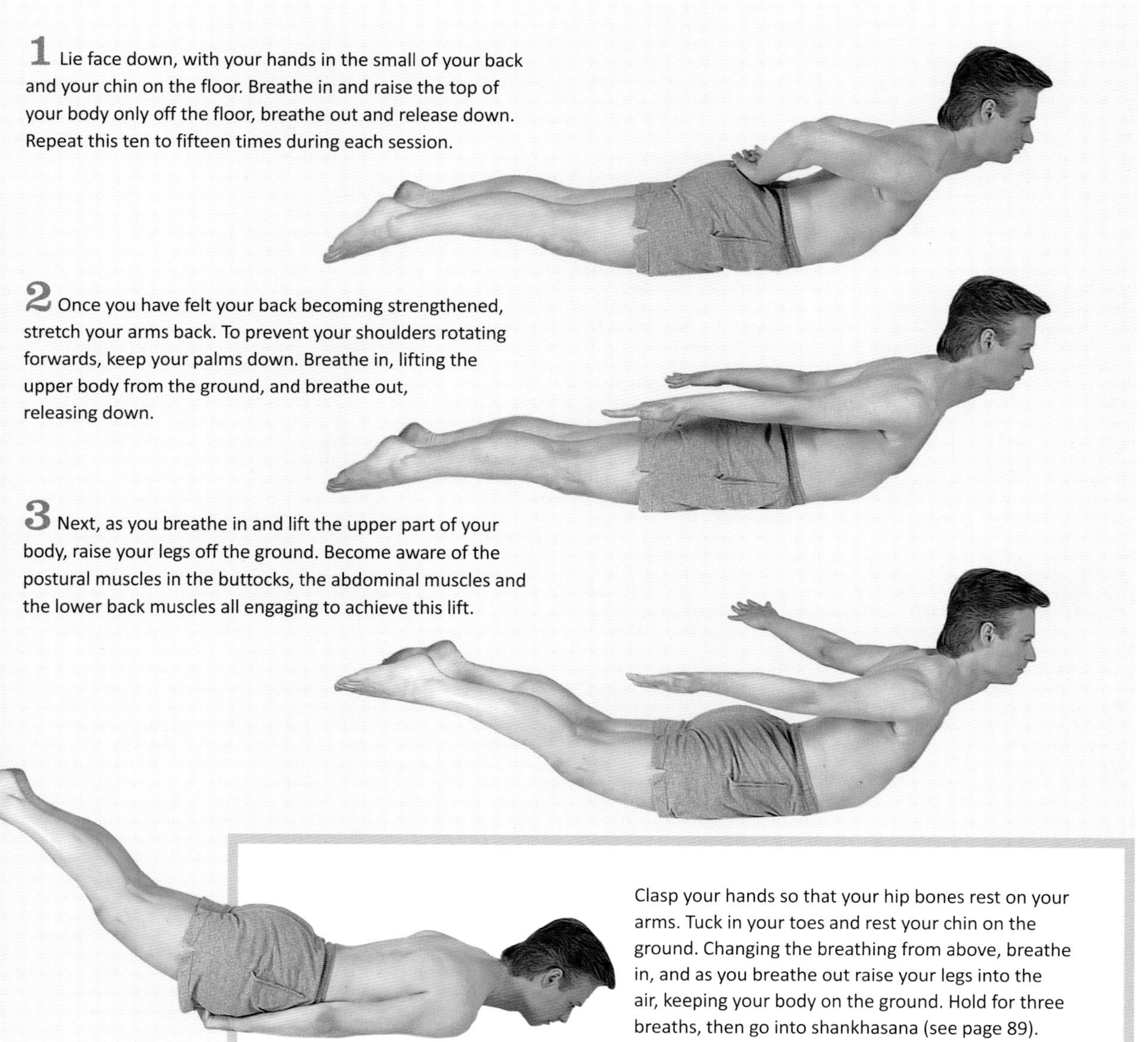

1 Lie face down, with your hands in the small of your back and your chin on the floor. Breathe in and raise the top of your body only off the floor, breathe out and release down. Repeat this ten to fifteen times during each session.

2 Once you have felt your back becoming strengthened, stretch your arms back. To prevent your shoulders rotating forwards, keep your palms down. Breathe in, lifting the upper body from the ground, and breathe out, releasing down.

3 Next, as you breathe in and lift the upper part of your body, raise your legs off the ground. Become aware of the postural muscles in the buttocks, the abdominal muscles and the lower back muscles all engaging to achieve this lift.

Clasp your hands so that your hip bones rest on your arms. Tuck in your toes and rest your chin on the ground. Changing the breathing from above, breathe in, and as you breathe out raise your legs into the air, keeping your body on the ground. Hold for three breaths, then go into shankhasana (see page 89).

BAKĀSANA

Crow posture

It's the creatures of the air that can revive the pranic flow of Apas Tattva, which, like water, tends always to flow downwards. To encourage an upward flow of this vitality, we look to the flight of locusts and birds. One of the problems of Apas Tattva is a tendency towards tamas. In order to counter this tendency, we employ postures that, while requiring a downward flow of weight in order to maintain balance, also call upon a grace and lightness to give lift.

If you are unable to find the balance point using the first method, shown on this page, try the variation of bakasana shown opposite. This posture takes time to achieve. Give yourself that time, letting your body feel its way to the confidence of balance.

1 From tadasana (see page 40), go into a forward bend and place the hands firmly on the floor about a foot in front of your feet. Bend your knees and, raising your feet, begin to rest the knees on the upper arm just above the elbows. In this part of the asana, you are feeling your way towards balance. Give yourself time here to enjoy this exploration rather than rushing towards the next part of the posture.

2 Allow your chin to lift, making the head a counterweight. As you explore your point of gravity, slowly allow your feet to lift off the floor. Hold the posture, maintaining muscle tone, but not tension, in the shoulders, and observe the body organizing itself around the posture, while also observing your breathing. Hold for two or three breaths, then release.

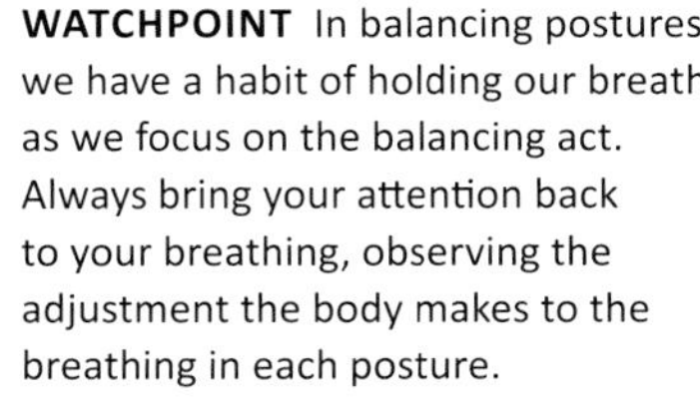

WATCHPOINT In balancing postures, we have a habit of holding our breath as we focus on the balancing act. Always bring your attention back to your breathing, observing the adjustment the body makes to the breathing in each posture.

VARIATION

1 Kneel down and place the crown of your head on a folded mat and your hands firmly on the floor, with the upper and lower arms forming a right angle.

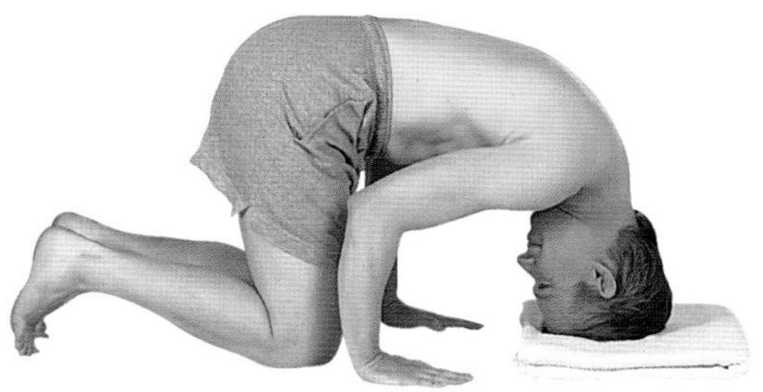

2 Straighten your legs and slowly walk towards your head until you feel that point of balance.

3 Now rest your knees on your upper arms just above the elbows.

4 As your body becomes balanced, slowly raise your feet off the ground and hold the posture. Concentrate on your breathing. Hold for five to ten breaths.

YOGA MUDRĀ

The gesture of the yogi

Once the asanas for Apas Tattva have been completed, assume yoga mudra to allow the vitality time to organize itself around these asanas that have opened and balanced channels of its flow. Remember that the inner attitude adopted in the postures is as important as the external. Allow an attitude of reverence to fill your whole being as you adopt this posture. The prana is distilled in the body during this posture, not flowing outwards or inwards, and it will become imbued with the stuff of your mind and of your emotions. Allow feelings and thoughts of the self as sacred and living within you to flow and enter every cell of your being as you surrender to the posture.

1 Assume padmasana (see page 93) and take hold of your toes. Breathe in, and as you breathe out drop your forehead onto the floor. Maintain this posture for about twelve breaths. If you are unable to adopt padmasana, go into easy posture (see page 65) and repeat as above.

2 Before releasing the posture, clasp your hands behind you and reach upwards – stretching and opening the front of the body while maintaining a forward bend. Release your arms, slowly come back up into a sitting posture and release.

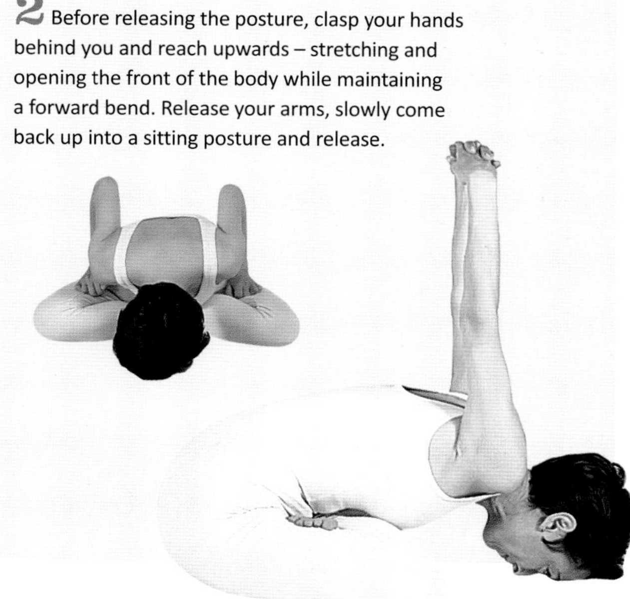

FURTHER TECHNIQUES

MUDRĀ

Svadhisthana Chakra is the seat of our will and resolution. Holding this gesture concentrates the vitality in the chakra and gives us the strength to remove obstacles to our continued growth. This is the chakra that seeks to create and re-create us – the vitality that flows from it feeds the reproductive organs. Through this mudra we give this tattva the strength and command to continue to hold what we need to continue our journey towards the light.

Sit in padmasana (see page 93). Hold the left hand down about four inches below the navel, palm facing upwards. Bring the right hand level with the navel, palm facing downwards. Allow the jaw, neck and shoulders to release and let your gaze drop to the floor. Observe the gentle flow of breath as the vitality of Apas is organized at Svadhisthana.

LIFESTYLE CONSIDERATIONS

Apas (water) and Prithvi (earth) Tattvas, governed by Svadhisthana and Muladhara Chakras, form the kapha (pronounced kappa) dosha of Ayurveda. Unlike the previous three tattvas, which tend to go into a rajasic state very easily (see 'The three gunas' on page 14), these two become tamasic very easily – leading to sluggishness and depression. We have to introduce movement – especially such as walking and vinyasa – into our daily routines to keep these balanced.

- The kapha dosha governs the lungs and breathing. Keeping this chakra balanced helps the entire respiratory function. Adding camphor oil to an oil disperser will help balance this chakra, as do foods such as pickled walnuts and garlic. However, avoid eating them in excess as they can make the whole energetic system tamasic. Add mint to hot water to make a balancing drink for this chakra.
- Find creative ways to add turmeric to your diet – its bitter and astringent taste is great for the digestive, circulatory and respiratory systems. In terms of energy, it can balance kapha if it has become tamasic and sluggish. It's highly effective in clearing all the meridians in the body and restoring the metabolism.

PRĀṆĀYĀMA

The phase of prana of this chakra is apana, the exhalation. This is an extremely important part of the entire respiratory cycle – unless the out-breath is full and complete, the inhalation cannot be. The yogis came up with a wonderful ratio for breath: 1:4:2. If we breathe in for the count of 1, we should breathe out for the count of 4, and the breath should be held out for the count of 2. This accords with the way the body absorbs oxygen from the red blood cells that have picked it up from the lungs. For the oxygen to be disengaged from the red blood cells, adequate levels of carbon dioxide need to be present in the plasma in which they are floating. If you are breathing in and out to the same count, you are technically hyperventilating – taking in oxygen in excess of the carbon dioxide being produced. The carbon dioxide levels then become lowered and the oxygen isn't able to get from the red blood cells to the body tissue as efficiently. My students and I work towards a ratio of 4:16:8. It's not possible to achieve this overnight, however – you need to begin slowly, and build up gradually towards the ratio.

EXERCISE

Sit in a comfortable position, with the weight releasing down. Use a chair if you aren't able to sit comfortably on the floor without collapsing at the abdomen.

- Start by counting your inhalations and then your exhalations, to determine your current breathing rate.
- Next, begin by increasing the count of the out-breath by just two.
- Gradually add to that until the out-breath is double that of the in-breath. Practise at this level for a couple of months and then gradually begin to increase it again.
- You will notice that, as you increase the duration of the exhalation, the duration of the stillpoint between breaths naturally increases. This stillpoint is a valuable time for the body, as it's when carbon dioxide levels are evened off.

MANTRA

'VAM'

VISUALIZATION

Again, imagine yourself beside the lake that has become your own private sanctuary. Give yourself time to become accustomed to being there. Now it's early evening – an auspicious time, known as the *brahmamahurta*, dusk. It corresponds to the predawn time of Vayu Tattva, which is also a brahmamahurta. The birds have all but stopped their chatter, and the wooded area around the lake is silent and expectant before the night activity begins. Remain still for a while, just breathing in this silence. Look out across the lake. There are the three lotus flowers in full bloom: the sixteen-petalled smoky-coloured lotus that reflects the full moon in its centre, the twelve-petalled golden lotus with the strange luminescent light glowing in its centre, and the ten-petalled yellow lotus with the fiery triangle in the centre. Something disrupts the smooth surface of the water, and a fountain of water breaks through. As it dies back down, it leaves a vermilion-petalled lotus with a dark centre in which is a shining crescent moon. Visualize yourself reaching forwards and scooping up the crystal-clear water. Bring the water to your mouth and drink it, lingering over its sweet taste. As the water enters you, feel its healing essence flowing through you, awakening your creative energies. As the lotus opens, it releases its deep sound that rolls across the water and enters you: Om Vam Om.

Situated at the perineum, between the genitals and the anus, Muladhara Chakra is the focus of Prithvi Tattva – the power of earth, with its call 'to be'. Finally, in this chakra the mature person walks steadily towards their destiny. The flower has become the fruit whose seeds will return to the earth and await germination. Here, at the root of sushumna nadi, where this golden pathway anchors itself in the deep earth of this chakra, we find our deepest and most basic potential: to be awakened to a full life in which all aspects of our being – physical, mental and spiritual – are incorporated.

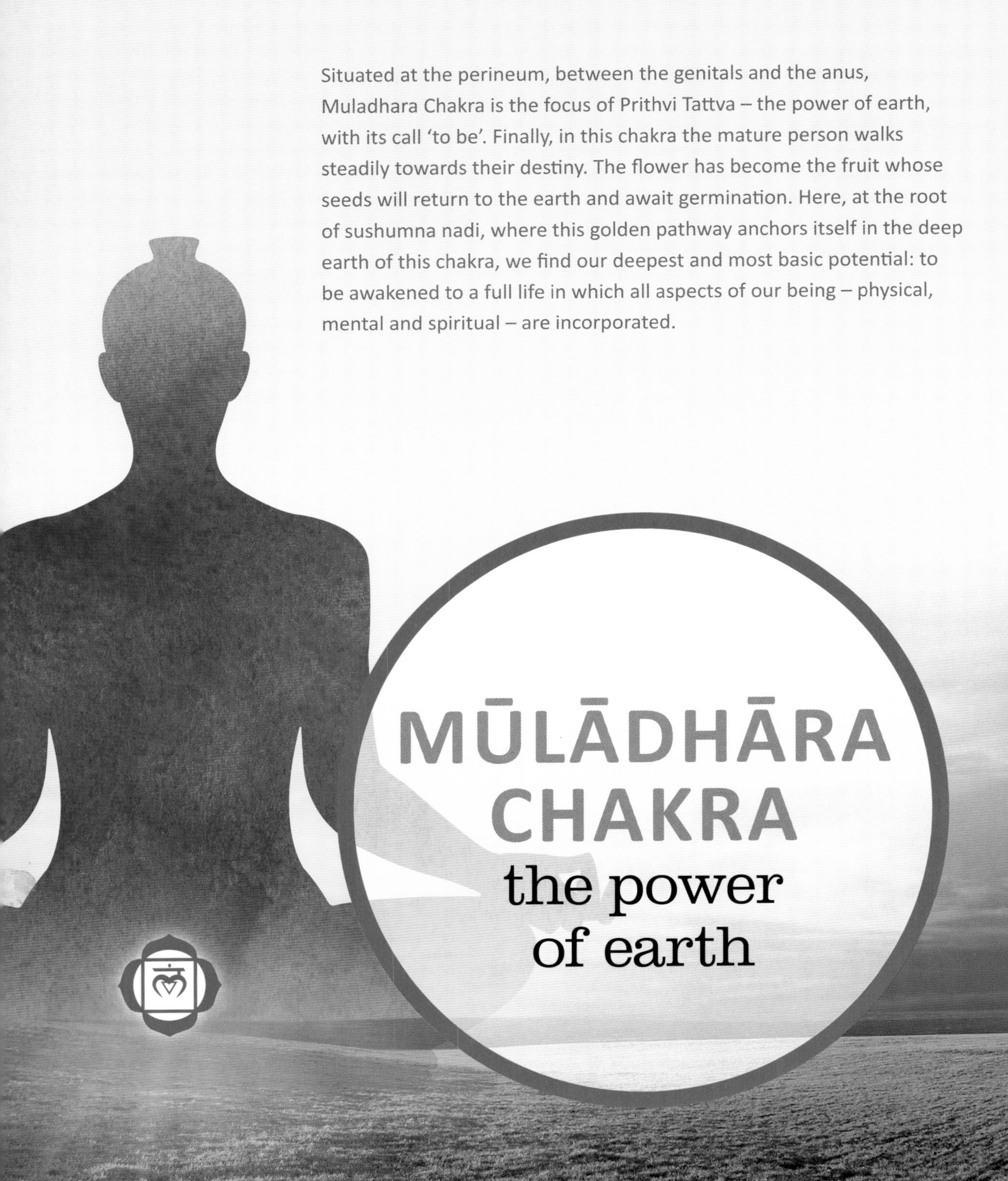

MŪLĀDHĀRA CHAKRA

the power of earth

PRANIC PHASE

Here we find the last of the five pranic phases, *udana* – the prana responsible for our speech and all movement that takes us upwards, returning us to that 'universal self'. Thus yoga, and particularly hatha yoga, isn't a 'restraint' of the vitality as some have suggested, but a complete and total realization of it. The powerful kundalini, coiled around the sacred lingam form of Shiva – must begin her ascent up sushumna to be once again united with Shiva at the crown. Here, in the rich dark earth, lies the power to move us upwards, back to our true nature.

EFFECT ON MIND AND BODY

This is the prana that nourishes the skeletal system – the muscles and joints of the body – and gives it stability and cohesion. Becoming aware of the integrity in bone, joint, muscle and movement is the full awakening of this chakra – and this is truly the business of the yogi. In honouring gravity, the pull towards earth, we take full responsibility for a vital part of our lives in which muscles work to hold us upright against a force that seeks to draw us down. We need to be integrated with both the downwards force and the movement upwards – then we become grounded enough to move in any direction we choose.

A complex system of some 600 muscles surrounds and attaches to the bones of our skeletal system and joints, giving us the option of movement. More than any other system in the body, it's the musculature that enacts the will. It's the musculature that responds to our desire to complete our asana practice or stay slouched on the couch in front of the television. But, like all our bodily systems, it responds quickly to our environment and can soon imprison the will as muscles tighten and joints stiffen. When this chakra becomes tamasic, we experience a loss of balance and equilibrium throughout our whole physical and psychological being. A sense of direction and purpose becomes confused with social directives. In a rajasic state, this chakra will cause us to become bound by anxieties and tensions. This can lead to a loss of movement that in later life will become a loss of mass in both bone and muscle.

THIS CHAKRA IN ASCENDANCY

If you are a person in whom this chakra is in ascendancy, you are supportive of other people's wants, dreams and ambitions. You will always have the desire to support and assist – ever ready with a good home-cooked meal. You will tend to keep your own concerns concealed while you listen to the problems of others. You will avoid any kind of conflict at all costs and will be quite unable to take sides in an argument. Rather, you will work energetically towards a resolution of the conflict as you support both sides.

ESSENTIAL PRITHVI TYPE

The essential Prithvi type is the diplomat, who is able to unify forces opposed to each other. With a keen desire to see everyone on earth supported and cared for, earth people will bring all their considerable resources (they have easier access to the other chakras than most others) to resolving the conflict. They will make people feel comfortable in their presence – comfortable with themselves as well as with their surroundings. No one is a stranger in the presence of an earth person.

BADDHA KOṆĀSANA

Bound angle posture

This posture is also known as kandasana. In Sanskrit, *kanda* is a bulbous or tuberous root. This asana works on our 'root' chakra – that which grounds us and keeps us stable and balanced. All of the preceding tattvas can be said to be rooted in Muladhara Chakra via sushumna nadi. Without descending fully into embodiment, we cannot reach for our divinity, for we reach for it via our practices – and to engage in these we need the physical body and both the intellectual and the intuitive mind.

It's in earth tattva most of all that we are able to understand the words of the avatar Bhagavan Shri Krishna when he said:

In any one part
All other parts are present
Like space being present in sound
Gross parts are present in the subtle
And the subtle unseen are present in the gross.

THE UDDHAVA GITA, DIALOGUE 17, VERSE 8

In kandasana, we are asked to release our weight down into the earth – to fully realize our rootedness on the earth, even while allowing the flow of prana from earth tattva at Muladhara Chakra to divinity to continue up sushumna nadi.

- Sit with your legs out in front of you, then bend the knees and draw the feet up so that the soles meet.
- Take hold of the feet with both hands and begin to release the weight down through the sitting bones.
- Allow the knees to release down. If your knees don't touch the ground, place folded towels under them – it's only possible for muscles to release when they feel support.
- Allow the spine to flow upwards – feel the front and back of the spine lengthening as the prana flows from Muladhara Chakra up to Sahasrara at the crown of the head.
- Allow the muscles at the back of the neck to lengthen and the shoulders to release and widen as you observe the breath.
- Hold for between five and fifteen breaths.

MERUDAṆḌĀSANA

Mountain staff posture

In this wonderful balancing posture we combine balance and poise with trust in the support and ground we feel beneath us. Only by releasing our weight down through Muladhara Chakra can we achieve this posture. Before you begin the posture, ensure that there are no obstructions behind you, so that if you do roll back, all you experience is a gentle massage to the spine.

WATCHPOINT Be careful not to draw the shoulders up in tension. Continue to let them widen and open to accommodate the breath while the back of the neck continues to lengthen.

1 From baddha konasana, raise the knees and grasp the big toes with each hand. Rock back on to the ball of the sitting bones and the very base of the spine. Lengthen the muscles at the back of the neck and drop the chin slightly. Breathe in, and as you breathe out slowly straighten the legs.

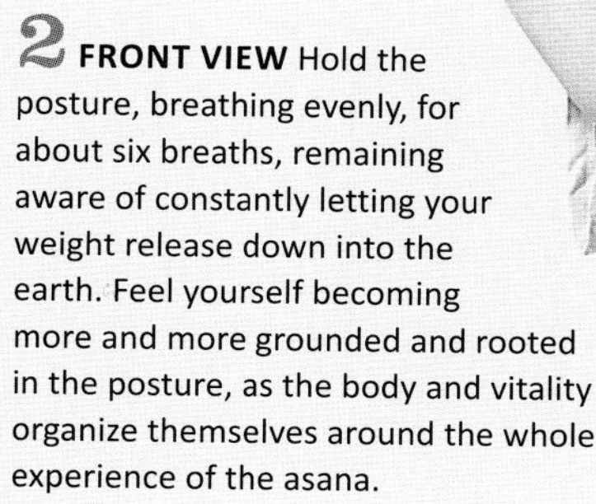

2 **FRONT VIEW** Hold the posture, breathing evenly, for about six breaths, remaining aware of constantly letting your weight release down into the earth. Feel yourself becoming more and more grounded and rooted in the posture, as the body and vitality organize themselves around the whole experience of the asana.

VĪRABHADRĀSANA III

Warrior III posture

Balancing postures act powerfully on Prithvi Tattva – it's when we are seeking balance that our support becomes active and awakened. Also, during the balancing postures we realize that until we feel supported we cannot find release or balance. In this posture we trust earth to continue to hold us up, while our muscles work both with and against the forces of gravity to allow us to move into – and explore – the space around us.

WATCHPOINT Don't let your body, head or hip rotate – this is a fear response. Learn to trust the power of one leg to take your weight. We often have to rely on slender things to assist us through crises in our lives. This posture gives us faith in the almost impossible.

1 Stand in tadasana (see page 40), releasing the weight down as you observe the breath. Once you feel the firmness of this posture, raise your arms and bring your palms together, clasping the middle, ring and little fingers together.

2 Breathe in, and as you breathe out allow whichever foot feels more natural to do so to take a step forwards. Let your weight fall down through that leg and continue down through the ankle, heel and instep into the earth. Let yourself become tall over this leg.

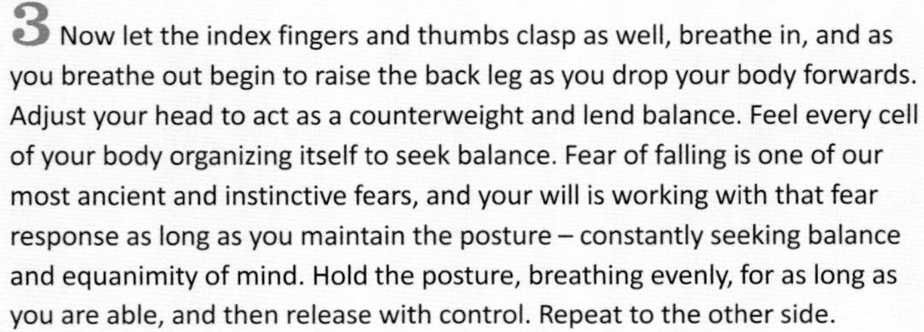

3 Now let the index fingers and thumbs clasp as well, breathe in, and as you breathe out begin to raise the back leg as you drop your body forwards. Adjust your head to act as a counterweight and lend balance. Feel every cell of your body organizing itself to seek balance. Fear of falling is one of our most ancient and instinctive fears, and your will is working with that fear response as long as you maintain the posture – constantly seeking balance and equanimity of mind. Hold the posture, breathing evenly, for as long as you are able, and then release with control. Repeat to the other side.

UPAVIṢTHA KOṆĀSANA

Seated angle posture

The entire pelvic basin – the seat of much tension and trauma – is also kanda: the root that nourishes and grounds us. If we store tension in this area, it becomes like a lid on our innate vitality. This posture opens muscles of the groin and lower back, giving the pelvic basin an opportunity to release its vitality into the body.

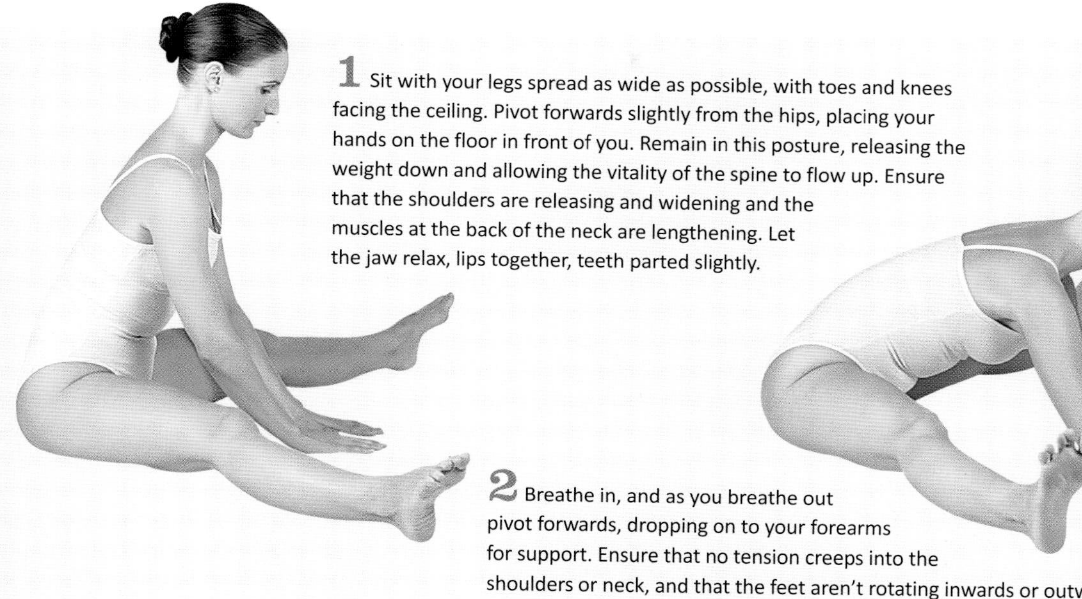

1 Sit with your legs spread as wide as possible, with toes and knees facing the ceiling. Pivot forwards slightly from the hips, placing your hands on the floor in front of you. Remain in this posture, releasing the weight down and allowing the vitality of the spine to flow up. Ensure that the shoulders are releasing and widening and the muscles at the back of the neck are lengthening. Let the jaw relax, lips together, teeth parted slightly.

2 Breathe in, and as you breathe out pivot forwards, dropping on to your forearms for support. Ensure that no tension creeps into the shoulders or neck, and that the feet aren't rotating inwards or outwards. (Rotation of the feet often indicates tension in the piriformis muscle in the buttocks – see page 124 for a stretch for this muscle.) Remain in this posture for a while, observing the movement of the breath in your back.

3 Engaging about ten per cent of your strength, draw the thigh muscles up towards the hips. This helps to stabilize the hips and gently pushes the back of the legs down into the floor. Allow the front of the spine to lengthen. Breathe in, and as you breathe out release your body down towards the floor. (If you are unable to reach the floor, place a bolster or rolled-up blanket on the floor to receive your body.) Let your chin rest on the floor as your hands reach out towards your feet. Let your shoulders release and lengthen. Feel the breath in your back – the muscles in the lower back expanding out to the sides as you breathe in, and releasing as you breathe out.

Remember: thirty per cent of the muscle is made up of connective tissue, which takes much longer to stretch than muscle tissue, so give your body time. Visualize the long muscles of the inner thigh lengthening and releasing; the muscles of the lower back giving up their tension; and the pelvis gently opening.

UTTHITA PĀRŚVA PĀDĀÑGUṢṬHĀSANA

Side toe stretch posture

Given that the tendencies of Vayu (air) and Agni (fire) are towards becoming rajasic, and Apas (water) and Prithvi (earth) towards becoming tamasic, we can employ the asanas to work against these tendencies. Fear of falling is primal and instinctive, and when we place the body in a demanding balancing posture, all of its resources become involved in keeping us upright. We don't have to consciously pull the body up – indeed, it's better not to interfere with its natural intelligence, but to observe that intelligence at work. It will employ exactly the right amount of muscle tone to keep us upright and balanced. In so doing, it draws prana that has been spiralling downwards and becoming too grounded – almost tamasic – upwards.

In this posture, Muladhara Chakra is opened as the pelvic floor and groin muscles are gently opened and lengthened. Manipura Chakra, which connects to the feet, is activated and calls upon the prana, drawing it into itself. Thus the entire system is gently awakened from a slumber, opened and energized.

- Stand in tadasana (see page 40).
- Take all your weight onto one leg and, as you release the weight down through that leg, feel your body growing tall over the leg as your spine lengthens.
- Bend the other knee and bring the foot up, taking hold of the big toe or the outside of the foot.
- Breathe in, and as you breathe out straighten the leg to the side.
- Breathe in, and as you breathe out raise the opposite arm to the same height as the arm holding the foot.
- Ensure that no tension has crept into your lower back, neck or jaw.

While you are holding the posture, feel the contact your hand is making with your foot, and the contact your other foot is making with the floor. Feel the whole length and width of your body. Observe the muscles in the leg supporting you, making minute adjustments to keep you up, and marvel at those movements.

If you were to remove a supporting pillar from a building, it would take months of labour to work out how to change the supporting structures to cope with that removal – your body makes these calculations and acts on them in microseconds! We are all great mathematicians.

PĀRŚVA KOṆĀSANA

Side angle posture

Antaeus, the son of Poseidon in Greek mythology, couldn't be defeated in battle. As soon as a blow felled him and he lay on the earth, he would be filled with life and vitality again. The hero Hercules is said to have conquered Antaeus by holding him aloft, out of touch with the earth, and thus draining the life out of him. Through the buildings and structures we create, we too are being held aloft and the vitality is being drained from us.

To reconnect with the earth and revitalize ourselves we need to learn to yield to gravity, the force of earth, even while we reach upwards. This posture gives us the perfect opportunity to do this.

1 Stand with your feet roughly four feet apart on a non-slip surface. Raise your arms to shoulder height, letting your shoulders remain released and widened and the back of your neck lengthened. Observe your breath.

2 Breathe in, and as you breathe out begin to bend one knee (start with whichever side feels more natural to you). Without strain, allow yourself to yield to gravity – slowly sinking down until your thigh is parallel to the floor. Ensure that the knee doesn't jut out over the ankle joint, but that both are in a straight line, forming a right angle with the foot. Reach down with the hand on the corresponding side and place it firmly on the floor.

BACK VIEW Feel the lines of vitality created by the asana.

3 Reach overhead so that your left arm, body and leg form a straight line. Ensure that the sacrum (lower back) remains tucked in and the shoulders released, not hunched. Hold for at least six breaths; observe the pelvic basin opening. Repeat to other side.

WATCHPOINT If you are unable to reach the floor with your hand, place a firm block or stool behind your foot and rest your hand on that.

SANĀTANĀSANA

Eternal posture

This posture is extremely difficult to hold for more than a few seconds, and yet it's called the 'eternal posture'! While we honour earth and the boundaries of time and space that it imposes on our being, we also have to break free of it – to go beyond matter and the limitations of maya, and discover the eternal in the present. To do that we have to go inwards – we have to be brave enough to look around inside ourselves and harness all that we have on the quest for the true, eternal self. This posture creates a perfect moment of extreme pressure as the whole being engages in keeping us upright – what better moment to discover what it means to be fully engaged on a quest? Simply remaining seated in padmasana can give the mind ample opportunity to meander through every thought that rolls through the consciousness. Here, every effort, every thought, is put at the disposal of remaining straight in a crooked position. It's within these paradoxes that the truth is able to reveal itself.

To remain whole, be twisted!
To become straight, let yourself be bent.
To become full, be hollow.
Be tattered in order to be renewed.

TAO TE CHING, LAO TZU

1 Sit in padmasana (see page 93) and observe your breathing for a while, allowing your spine to flow upwards. Experience the flow of energy through the body in this stable posture.

2 Push up and forwards and take your weight onto your knees, with your hands assisting in the balance by being in touch with the floor in front of you. Don't take your consciousness off your breathing – allow it to flow freely.

3 Breathe in, and as you breathe out let go of the earth and reach up with your entire body, bringing your hands into a prayer position. Hold for as long as you are able, all the while attempting to be conscious of how the body–mind complex has engaged itself in the asana.

GARUḌĀSANA

Sacred eagle posture

Garuda is the sacred eagle who acts as a carrier and messenger of the god Vishnu in Hindu mythology. In this posture, we allow the body to emulate the waiting Garuda – the Garuda who is earthbound with folded wings but whose focus is on the world beyond this one as he waits for the call when he will spread his wings and fly, breaking free of gravity. Thus, with the body we emulate our spiritual journey: rooted to earth and aware of the world of matter, we fix our attention on our divine nature.

Special attention has to be placed on the pelvic basin in this posture. It's easy to tip the pelvis to one side or the other as you go into it. When standing in tadasana to begin, visualize the pelvic basin as being a basin full of warm water. Is it level or is the water splashing over the edge? Make the minute adjustments you need to until you feel the the pelvis is steady and symmetrical.

FRONT VIEW

- Stand in tadasana (see page 40).
- Take your weight over onto one foot and allow yourself to become tall over that foot.
- Breathe in, and as you breathe out slowly bend the knee slightly so that the weight is going through the bent leg. Ensure that the spine is still lengthening upwards and has not slumped.
- Breathe in, and as you breathe out slowly bring the opposite leg up and wrap it round the leg holding your weight. Think of a bird balancing on one leg.
- Breathe in, and as you breathe out raise the arm on the same side as the leg you have raised, and bend the elbow.
- Breathe in, and as you breathe out wrap the other hand around the raised arm, tucking the elbow inside, so that the fingers of the raised hand touch the palms of the hand you have wrapped around it.
- Hold for five to twelve breaths. Repeat to the other side.

SIDE VIEW

- The hands will be obscuring your gaze; you should be looking directly into them as they align with the centre of the face.
- Be aware of not lifting the tailbone and thus shortening the spine.
- In balancing postures it's easy to suspend the breath. Remain aware of the breath, keeping it non-reactive and flowing evenly.
- You may find it helpful to visualize the image of a bird tucking its head into its feathers for rest.

KAPOTĀSANA

Dove posture

The bird imagery helps us greatly in opening and balancing Prithvi Tattva. Like us, birds are bound to the earth's atmosphere by gravity, and yet they alight on earth and take off from it again. The same should apply to us – remember the words of Krishna: 'the gross is present in the subtle and the subtle unseen is present in the gross'. Our practice as yogis and yoginis is to see the divine in the material. That's to say, we have to have knowledge of the tattvas, to see them all as the 'isms' of the divine. Then, like birds, we are not bound to matter any more than matter is bound to the earth – we are free to soar.

1 Sit on the ground, with the left foot resting against the groin and the right foot placed behind. Release your weight down. You may become aware that one buttock is slightly raised. Don't try to force it down. Continue to be aware of releasing your weight through the sitting bones into the earth and it will slowly, in its own time, level out.

2 Turn your body to face your left knee, which remains bent, and begin to straighten your right leg behind you, thigh facing down. Hold this posture for a few minutes, lengthening through the front of your spine and enjoying the sensation of the front of the left hip gently opening.

3 Breathe in, and as you breathe out bend the right knee and bring the lower leg up to form a right angle with the thigh. Hold for a few breaths, then release.

The Patanjali *Yoga Sutras* begin with the Sanskrit word *atha*, which is usually translated as 'now'. Atha is what is known as a *mangala*, an auspicious sound, and the 'now' here denotes an auspicious moment. Give yourself time as you move into and out of postures to find the 'atha' – the auspicious moment for each transition. Watch your breath, and when that moment comes in this posture, gently slide the appropriate leg out from under the weight of the thigh.

4 Now extend the right leg behind you again, even further this time. As you release your weight down, stretch up from deep within your abdomen. Hold the posture, breathing.

5 When you are ready to release, slowly let your body pivot forwards and allow your forehead to come to rest on the ground as your arms stretch forwards and also rest on the floor. This is an extreme flexion for the hip and knee joints, and you should come out of the position immediately if you feel any discomfort. If it does feel comfortable, hold it for a few seconds and then sit up and assume the posture you began with. The hip and knee joints will then both be flooded with a fresh supply of nourishment. Remember: cartilage doesn't have its own blood supply but is nourished by blood when the joint is taken into full flexion or extension. When you feel ready, repeat to the other side.

SUPTA VĪRĀSĀNA

Reclining hero's posture

Beginning on both sides of the spine at the twelfth thoracic vertebrae is the powerful iliopsoas muscle. Attaching to all the lumbar vertebrae and continuing down to mingle with fibres that are anchored to the inner surface of the pelvis, it then descends to attach to the top of the thigh bones. It lifts the upper leg in a movement known as 'flexion of the hip'. We cannot take a step without it.

While fear is generally a healthy response – it makes us respond to danger – the iliopsoas can be especially susceptible to 'muscle armouring' (when continuous low levels of anxiety and fear lock into our muscles), giving rise to a wide range of symptoms, from back ache to hip and leg pain. Tension here can affect our gait and, gradually, the smooth flow of communication from earth to body is diminished.

This posture, repeated slowly over time until the body is able to release down fully onto the floor, stretches and releases this muscle, allowing it to let go of its tension.

1 Sit in vajrasana (see page 39), with your big toes touching, observing the breath.

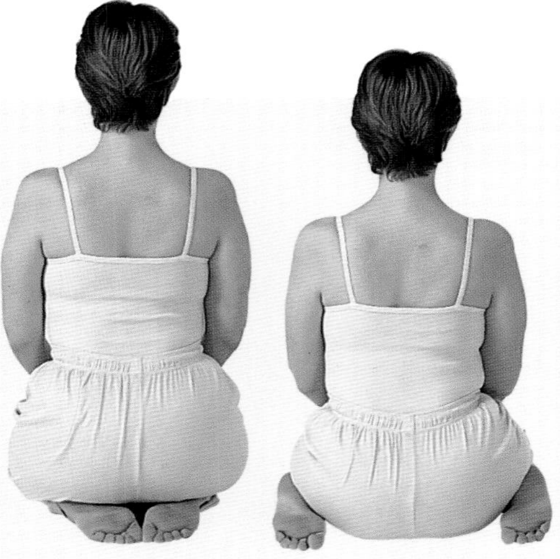

2 Slide your lower legs outwards and place your feet alongside your buttocks. Let your weight release down into the floor through your sitting bones.

3 Take your hands behind you, fingers pointing towards the buttocks, and slowly lower yourself onto your elbows. Don't let your head drop back. Breathe in, and as you breathe out slowly move your elbows aside and let your body release onto the floor.

4 With the next breath, as you breathe out raise your arms overhead and, stretching up, release them into the floor. Focus on the feeling of the entire front of the body being open and receptive, while the weight of the body releases down through your points of contact with the ground, into the earth. Hold for three or four breaths, then release the legs and hug them into the chest.

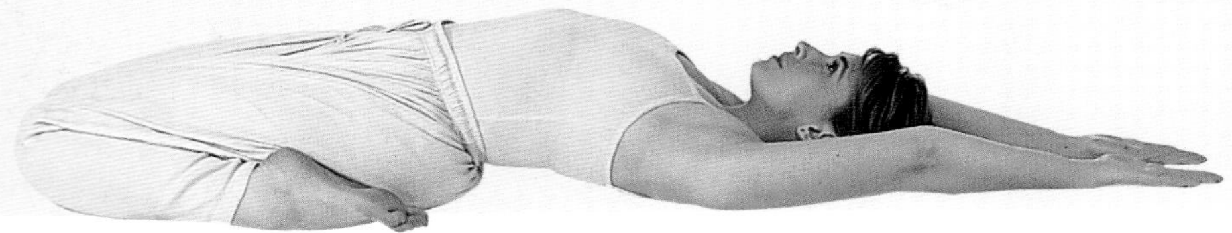

MŪLĀBANDHA

Root bandha

This is one of the most simple but profound of all the bandhas. To understand its significance the practitioner needs a deeper understanding of Muladhara Chakra. Each chakra has unique symbols to give us this deeper understanding and insight. Each also has a particular *devi* (goddess) and *deva* (god) presiding over it, and an animal – usually mythical – associated with it. The devi presiding over mulabandha is Savitri – a daughter of the sun and the wife of Brahma, the progenitor of creation (she's also known as Dakini). The mythology of creation says that after Brahma had fashioned the universe he placed his seed in Savitri, and after a hundred years she gave birth to the Vedas – the ancient books that contain all knowledge and divine wisdom. She rides the white four-tusked elephant Airavata, who is the mount of Indra, king of the heavens. Airavata is the body that's the vehicle of conscious wisdom, Savitri.

Similarly, the earth chakra is the supporter of all the other tattvas. Rooted deep within it is sushumna nadi, which flows up the centre of the spine to reach the thousand-petalled lotus at the crown of the head. Also taking root in Muladhara are the ida nadi and pingala nadi – the 'ha' and 'tha' of hatha yoga ('ha' signifying the expansive nature of prana, symbolized by the sun, and 'tha' signifying its contractive nature, symbolized by the moon). The hatha yogi's practices aim at balancing these two forces. All embrace the sacred lingam form of Shiva – around which is coiled the focus of the yoga practitioner's attention, the kundalini. She's depicted as a snake – divine consciousness manifest. Awakening this slumbering force, and drawing it up to Sahasrara at the crown of the head, is the primary objective of hatha yoga. Mulabandha is one of the most powerful ways to do this, and to realize our full potential.

PREPARATORY EXERCISE

- Sit in padmasana (see page 93), or, if this isn't possible for you, in easy posture (see page 65).
- Become aware of the contact you have with the ground at the perineum.
- Before you attempt mulabandha, work with the muscles in this region to become accustomed to them. Breathe in and draw all the muscles of the pelvic basin upwards towards the navel. Hold them there for a few seconds, then release and exhale.
- When you have done this a few times, move your attention to the muscles around the rectum. Try to isolate these and draw them up towards the navel as you inhale. Hold and release. Repeat a few times.
- Next, focus your attention on the muscles just around your genitalia and draw them up as you breathe in, then release. Repeat a few times.

MŪLĀBANDHA

Once you have done the above exercise, you are ready to try mulabandha.

- Remain in padmasana or your chosen sitting position.
- Breathe in and locate the muscles at the area between the anus and genitalia, and draw these muscles up towards the navel.
- Hold the muscles in this drawn position and feel that all the vitality is flowing up towards Agni Tattva at Manipura Chakra.
- Simultaneously, feel that the vitality of the inhalation is flowing down into Manipura Chakra, and that the power of Agni is transforming these two vitalities that are meeting there.
- As you release this powerful bandha, feel the transformed vitality descend down into Muladhara Chakra to strike the slumbering kundalini into full wakefulness.

FURTHER TECHNIQUES

MUDRĀ

In this gesture we come to the full realization of ourselves as a single spiritual being. We employ intellectual knowledge (bauddha jnana) that we have gained on our journey and intuitive knowledge (paurusha jnana) that we have developed through our evolution. From here we return to the source – the journey's end. It's Paurusha Jnana that will lead us to that final *moksha* (liberation) in which we realize our oneness with all. Then we may be *aware* of the body, mind and personality but not *identified* with them.

Sit in padmasana (see page 93), with your hands resting on your thighs, your fingers arranged in jnana mudra – the gesture of knowledge. Bend your index fingers so that the tips are in contact with the base of the thumb. Fix your gaze on the floor in front of you and observe the breath and the thoughts flowing through your consciousness.

LIFESTYLE CONSIDERATIONS

Prithvi (earth) is the tattva that holds all the others together. Like the earth, it gives stability and cohesion. It's here, residing in a slumbering state, that we find our most powerful urge towards meaning and spirituality – what the ancients called kundalini. This tattva gives us balance and a sense of groundedness. We honour its energy by giving support to the projects that we develop through the energy of the other chakras. There's a tendency with this chakra to always put others first. Nurturing others is natural to us and part of the gift of this chakra, but we can exhaust it by not honouring ourselves as much as we do others.

- Here, bone and muscle must be fed with a diet that's rich in minerals such as magnesium, calcium and trace minerals, ensuring we get the vitamin D_3 that natural sunshine offers. Bone and muscle are also built through movement – and for those with sedentary desk jobs, building in a movement and exercise programme is essential.
- In Ayurveda, Prithvi (earth) and Apas (water) form kapha dosha – the dosha that tends towards heaviness and sluggishness. Adding things like parsley and pomegranate to salads will help to keep this dosha balanced. Adding myrrh and frankincense to an oil diffuser will also enhance the energy of this chakra.

PRĀṆĀYĀMA

The phase prana enters here is udana – that which returns our vitality to an upwards flow to form speech, and which calls the kundalini to enter sushumna and rise towards Sahasrara. Now we can enter the stillpoint most deeply. Having extended the out-breath and balanced the flow of oxygen and carbon dioxide in your body, you may enter into the stillpoint with full attention.

EXERCISE

Sit in easy posture (see page 65) and release the weight down through the body and points of contact with the ground.

- Release and widen the shoulders as you breathe, and let the muscles of the neck lengthen. Let your jaw relax. Don't count your breathing – let it flow, but observe it all the while.
- Feel the cool air enter your nostrils, hit the back of the throat and descend into the body. Then feel the warm air rising up through the throat, leaving through the nose as you breathe out.
- Fix your attention on the exhalation and the stillpoint between exhalation and inhalation. Watch for the movement that gives rise to the next breath. Let yourself be drawn ever deeper into that stillpoint.
- Don't try to hold the stillpoint. Let it have a natural duration and allow your consciousness to be drawn more deeply into each stillpoint. It's in the motionlessness of the stillpoint that the self is revealed.

MANTRA

'LAM'

VISUALIZATION

You are beside the lake in the depth of night. It's impossible to see where the lake ends and the shore begins; where you end and the night begins. Don't be afraid of this loss of boundary – let yourself enter into it. Feel your weight releasing down into the earth as you become part of it. Each time you breathe in, you inhale millions of molecules. Some of these molecules are particles of other breathing beings that have lived on the planet. With each inhalation, feel yourself connected to the past as you draw the breath and this past into yourself. Each time you breathe out, you exhale millions of molecules. These will remain on earth as long as our atmosphere remains. As you breathe out, feel that you are connected with the future through the out-breath. All you can see is the white light of the full moon from the Vishuddha lotus, the soft glow from the Anahata lotus, the fiery triangle from the Manipura lotus and the sliver of light from the crescent moon of the Svadhisthana lotus. Watch the final lotus with its blood-red petals emerge from the water with the yellow square in its centre.

Visualize a radiant hollow tube running from your perineum up your spine to the crown of your head. Breathe in – feel a cool current flow down this tube. Breathe out and feel a warm current rise up it. Watch this tube grow more radiant with each breath, and see the lotus on the water's surface appearing within it. At the perineum, see the four red petals of Muladhara lotus with its yellow square at the centre. Listen to its sound within you: Om Lam Om. At the base of the spine, see the six vermilion petals of Svadhisthana lotus with the crescent moon in its centre. Let its sound resonate through you: Om Vam Om. Behind your navel see the ten yellow petals of Manipura lotus with its fiery triangle in the centre. Hear its sound flow through you: Om Ram Om. Behind the heart is the Anahata lotus with its twelve golden petals, and in its smoky interior is the strange and mysterious glow of light. Let its sound enter each cell: Om Yam Om. At the base of your throat see the sixteen smoky petals of the Vishuddha lotus with the full moon in its dark centre. Let its soft sound descend and rise: Om Ham Om. Between the eyebrows is the white two-petalled lotus of Ajna Chakra in which lies the blue pearl of consciousness. Listen carefully to its sound, the sacred pranava mantra, Om. Above that the fullness of Brahman – the expansion, the infinity that you are. Feel now that everything in the universe is reflected in you. That you are an essential and necessary part of a whole that continues to expand outwards, ever outwards; and that the universe – even at its outermost boundaries – is lovingly aware of your presence.

INTEGRATION

Each of the seven chakras, from Sahasrara at the crown of the head down to Muladhara at the perineum, represents our descent from wholeness into this slippery world of samsara and duality. We didn't come to it all at once and we won't return all at once. Our return to our own true nature will also be an evolution. This is why the sage Patanjali gave us the eight-point programme of ashtanga yoga. Understanding that the realization of oneness is an evolution, he broke it down into a system.

Hatha yoga – specifically asana and pranayama – is the first two steps of that return to our true nature. When done with an internal focus, these practices train us to take the next necessary steps: to deal with the world while maintaining a set of values, and to value ourselves enough to maintain a lifestyle conducive to a return through the niyama and yama. Once we know ourselves well enough through our practice and are restored to a life purpose, we can understand how important these personal and social values are.

Continuing in this practice, then, draws us along this evolutionary pathway, and we naturally and effortlessly enter into pratyahara and dharana – withdrawal from external stimulation to internal awareness and focused concentration. Holding a posture while remaining aware is still one of the best methods that I have encountered for learning concentration. Because it engages the body, it makes it possible for the mind to become alert, rather than distracted. But these evolutionary stages only hold true so long as we don't approach our yoga practice as an exercise of will over body. Dhyana and that final stage of evolution, samadhi, require a complete surrender of personality that also has to be practised, to be 'felt' as a bodily event. As we surrender the will and observe the resistance embodied in muscles, tendons and joints, we begin to understand what it means to yield.

INTEGRATING THE FIVE TATTVAS

A number of postures lend themselves well to experiencing an integration of the five tattvas. Best among these are the vinyasa – sequences of postures – rather than a holding of one particular posture. The focus is within: as you watch your body move through the sequence, you allow the mind to become still. Most famous of all vinyasas is surya namaskar (salute to the sun), included in this section. There are also two other sequences you can do either at the beginning or the end of your asana practice. While doing them, remember these stages of evolution and, as you move your body through the sequences, let your mind begin to organize itself around the possibility that it need not get 'stuck' in any one mode of thinking.

Remember that all these tattvas are within you. You are the priest who can conduct the perfect ritual; you are the warrior princess who can provide leadership; you are the healer and entertainer who will charge everything with magic; you are the dreamer and truth seeker; and you are the diplomat and negotiator, always seeking to bring together the disparate. All these qualities reside in you – allow your mind to move freely among them and use what is appropriate. Only when the mind is given this kind of freedom will it find within itself the ability to become fixed in meditative concentration (dhyana), necessary for that final stage, samadhi: liberation.

These asanas should be done with particular focus and care. They, especially, will untie the knots that the past has created and bring you into a free-flowing present. Enjoy them. When doing your yoga practice, always remember that what makes it different to many other physical exercises is intention. Yoga is the intention of the soul to return to its reality. Become fully awakened to that voice within that keeps telling you that you are much more than you can possibly imagine. Shake off the boundaries of the ahamkara that others have created for you, and allow yourself to walk this path of liberation.

SŪRYA NAMASKĀRA

Salute to the sun

Surya namaskar is a vinyasa – a sequence of asanas done without pausing between each one. It's an ancient vinyasa of yoga. Yoga, Ayurveda and Jyotish (Vedic) developed alongside each other in ancient India; surya namaskar pays homage to the twelve houses of Jyotish. The idea is that each morning the yogi would perform the twelve asanas of this vinyasa as a homage to the twelve houses in their natal chart, while verbally or mentally chanting the mantras – thus aligning their energies with the stars of their personal birthchart and aligning and integrating the tattvas of the body with the tattvas as they appear in the universe. There are twelve asanas in the vinyasa, each with its own name, energetic function and mantra.

PHYSICAL BENEFITS

This sequence bends the spine forwards and backwards, opening the front and back of the spine and remobilizing it. The sequence also stretches the long muscles of the back and the back of the legs in the forward bends, and the iliopsoas muscle (of the hip joint) in the backbends. In the second and eleventh asana, the pectoralis major muscle is gently stretched and the scapula is pressed in the serratus anterior and subscapularis muscles, giving them a gentle massage. However, the major benefit of this sequence is to the overall circulation – particularly the lymph system, which is sluggish during sleep, when muscles are relatively inactive.

FIRST ASANA

Praṇamasana I

(standing prayer posture)

Stand with your feet hip distance apart (the heels under the head of the femur). Release the weight through your body, allow your shoulders to release and widen, the muscles at the back of your neck to lengthen and your jaw to release. On an out-breath, bring the palms together in front of the heart. Focus your attention on bringing the left and right sides of your energetic body into alignment and balance with each other as your palms meet over the centre of your being: your heart. This posture corresponds to the First House in Jyotish, **Thanu Bhava** – House of the Body. It's a 'dharma' house, connected to the life purpose. It will govern appearance, character and disposition as well as strength and longevity.

MANTRA

Om Mitrāya Namaḥ

(I greet the Friend of All)

SECOND ASANA

Hasta Uttānāsana (raised arm posture)

Keep your weight flowing down, contract the abdominal muscles to support the lower back and, as you breathe in, lengthen the whole spine, raising your arms until the forearm aligns with the ears, and go into a slight backbend. Feel the front of your spine lengthening and your chest opening. Having greeted the 'friend of all' you now open yourself wide, allowing its energy to penetrate you. When we raise our arms and leave our heart unprotected, we signal to energy that we are ready to receive and embrace it. This posture corresponds to the Second House of Jyotish, **Dhana Bhava** – House of Wealth. It's an 'artha' house, connected with wealth. It will govern finances, knowledge, education, speech and oration, domestic life and confidence.

MANTRA

Om Ravaye Namaḥ

(I greet the Shining One)

THIRD ASANA

Uttānāsana (hand to foot posture)

As you exhale, keep your arms extended above your head and move into a forward bend. Remember to keep your weight going down through your ankles and heels (not letting it come forwards to your toes). If you are unable to get the heels of your hands on the floor, bend your knees a little. If you just let your fingers touch the floor, or allow your hands to dangle in the air, the proprioceptors (your sensitive internal sensors) get the message of instability, and muscles will start to tense as they attempt to keep you upright. Once you are in the forward bend, let your head go, so that its weight can stretch the long muscles of the back. This posture corresponds to the Third House of Jyotish, **Sahaja Bhava** – House of Siblings. It's a 'kama' house, connected to desires. It will govern your efforts and adventures, brothers and sisters, and all the desires and ambitions you are born with.

MANTRA

Om Sūryāya Namaḥ

(I greet the Lord of the Sun, initiator of activity)

FOURTH ASANA

Aśva Saṁcalāsana (horse posture)

As you inhale, extend one leg back, bending the toes against the floor. At the same time raise your head and extend the front of your throat and neck, looking up. Place both hands at the sides of the foot that's still flat on the floor. This position corresponds to the Fourth House of Jyotish, **Sukha Bhava** – House of Happiness and Comforts. It's a 'moksha' house, connected with spiritual realization. It will govern the mother, your degree of contentment, emotions and education.

MANTRA

Om Bhavane Namaḥ

(I greet the One who illuminates the twelve astrological houses)

FIFTH ASANA

Dandāsana (staff posture)

MANTRA

Om Khagāya Namaḥ

(I greet the One who moves across the sky)

As you exhale, extend the other leg back so that it's in line with the first, straightening both legs and allowing the arms and hands to take the upper-body weight and the toes and feet to take the lower-body weight. Be sure to drop your buttocks to bring the entire body into a straight line. This posture corresponds to the Fifth House of Jyotish, **Putra Bhava** – House of Our Children. It's a 'dharma' house, connected to life purpose. It will govern children and grandchildren, the mind, rewards from past births, and your sense of destiny.

SIXTH ASANA

Aṣṭāñga Namaskāra (the eight-limbed salutation)

Lower your body onto the ground so that your toes, knees, chest, chin and hands are in contact with the ground and your buttocks are raised, lifting your tailbone. This is the Sixth House of Jyotish, **Satru Bhava** – House of Enemies. It's an 'artha' house, connected to wealth. It will govern health and illness, competitors and weaknesses, daily occupation, extended family and appetite.

MANTRA

Om Pūṣṇe Namaḥ

(I greet the One who cherishes and nourishes this world)

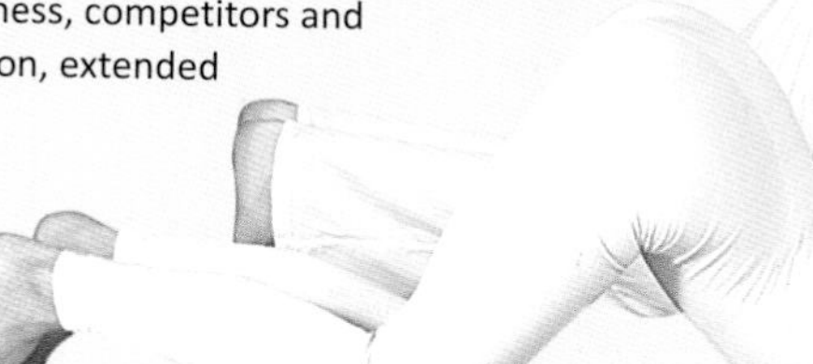

SEVENTH ASANA

Bhujañgāsana (cobra posture)

The heels of your hands should be directly under your shoulders. As you inhale, push up so that you rise off the floor like a cobra in strike position. The tops of your feet should remain flat on the floor and, once you are up to your own fullest stretch, you should be looking directly ahead, with the steady gaze of a cobra. This is the Seventh House of Jyotish, **Jaya Bhava** – House of One's Spouse. It's a 'kama' house, connected to desires. It will govern your spouse and married life, all your partners and sexual passions, and foreign travel.

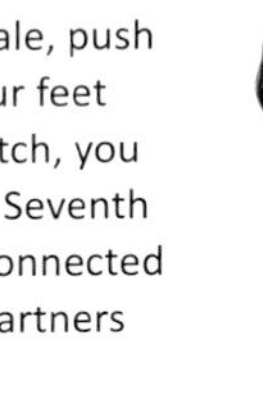

MANTRA

Om Hiraṇyagarbhāya Namaḥ

(I greet the Golden Embryo from which this universe emerges)

EIGHTH ASANA

Adho Mukha Śvānāsana I

(downward facing dog posture I)

MANTRA

Om Marīchāya Namaḥ

(I greet the Lord of the Dawn)

Release your body from bhujangasana and, as you exhale, take a small step forwards and push up into supreme mountain posture. The energy thrust should push up through the arms into the shoulder blades and take your buttocks back. Allow your head to release and become heavy, and drop your heels down into (or towards) the floor. This is the Eighth House of Jyotish, **Mrtyu Bhava** – House of Death. It's a 'moksha' house, connected with spiritual realization. It will govern longevity, as well as your partner's finances and the ability to generate wealth.

NINTH ASANA

Aśva Saṁcalāsana (horse posture)

MANTRA

Om Adityāya Namaḥ

(I greet the Son of Aditi – sovereign of the twelve months of my natal chart)

As you inhale, swing your leg forwards (the same leg that was forwards before), bringing the foot flat onto the floor and bending the knee so that the lower half of your leg is in line with your arms. At the same time, raise your chin, stretching the front of your neck and upper chest. Keep your hands in contact with the floor. This is the Ninth House of Jyotish, **Bhagya Bhava** – House of Fortune. It's a 'dharma' house, connected to our life purpose. It will govern the father, luck and fortunes, ability to solve problems, religion and philosophy, faith, guru, elders and wisdom.

TENTH ASANA

Uttānāsana (hand to foot posture)

As you exhale, bring the other leg forwards, drop your head and place the heels of your hands flat on the floor (as before, if you are unable to do this with your legs straight, then bend your knees). Remember to keep your weight going down through your ankles and heels, and adjust the position of your hips and buttocks so that the weight doesn't come forwards onto your toes, as this causes muscles throughout the structure to tense up. This is the Tenth House of Jyotish, **Karma Bhava** – House of Activities. It's an 'artha' house, connected to wealth. It will govern career and profession, fame, honour and status, worldly power, good deeds and prominent people in your life.

MANTRA

Om Savitre Namaḥ

(I greet the Benevolent Mother of All and protector of the day)

ELEVENTH ASANA

Hasta Uttānāsana (raised arm posture)

Keep your weight flowing down and, as you inhale, begin to straighten and raise your arms until the forearms align with the ears. Come straight up and then into a slight backbend, remembering to support the spine through the power of the abdominal muscles. Feel the front of your spine lengthening and your chest opening. Again, you stand unprotected before the dawn and the rising sun – signalling that you are prepared to be open and receive all that life will offer you. This is the Eleventh House of Jyotish, **Ayaya Bhava** – House of Gain. It's a 'kama' house, connected to desires. It will govern your major goals and ambitions, opportunities, profit and financial fluctuations, capital ventures and family elders.

MANTRA

OM Arkāya Namaḥ

(I greet the One whose radiance arcs across the sky)

TWELFTH ASANA

Praṇamasana I (standing prayer posture)

As you exhale, bring your hands down with your palms together over your heart. Now feel how much easier it is to bring all your energy into alignment, having gone through the sequence. Allow your weight to keep descending down through your legs, ankles, heels and into the floor. Keep your attention on holding your energy at this stillpoint before you begin the next sequence, swinging the opposite leg back first. This is the Twelfth House of Jyotish, **Vyaya Bhava** – House of Loss. It's a 'moksha' house, connected with spiritual realization. It will govern your expenditures and expenses, final spiritual liberation, state of affairs at death and plane of existence after it.

MANTRA

Om Bhāskarāya Namaḥ

(I greet the One who cherishes and nourishes this world)

ADHO MUKHA ŚVĀNĀSANA I

Downward facing dog posture I

Some postures by nature work so powerfully on reorganizing the spine and liberating it from habitual patterns of tension that the flow of prana throughout the back is improved. This asana is also known as sumeru yogasana, meaning 'sacred or supreme mountain pose'.

If you think of the spine as a column built on a foundation, it will become easier to understand spinal integration. Alignment of this column depends on the foundation – the sacrum – being in a balanced position. If the sacrum is tilting one way or the other because of a poor or compromised sacroiliac joint, the muscles around the entire column will adapt to accommodate this position. In order to release and integrate the entire spinal column and the flow of prana through it, its relationship with the sacrum and the sacroiliac joint must be addressed. Sumeru is a mythological mountain – abode of the gods – and in this posture we acquire a steadiness of both body and mind.

1 Go onto all fours, with the heels of your hands directly under the shoulders and your knees directly under the hips (not pressed together). Allow the spine to flow in a neutral position, and breathe in.

2 As you breathe out, push up through your arms and legs so that your buttocks are reaching upwards. Drop your head and heels towards the floor. When first attempting this posture don't let the body just 'hang' from the arms – instead, push up through your arms so that you feel the energy force right up into the shoulder blades and feel your back flattening. Allow the front of the thighs to push gently backwards – this will lengthen the muscles at the back of the legs and allow the heels to release down further. Hold the posture for about six breaths and then slowly release into shankhasana (see page 89) for about six breaths.

ADHO MUKHA ŚVĀNĀSANA II

Downward facing dog posture II

This posture doesn't feel quite as stable and steady as the version opposite, but it gives a greater stretch to the muscles of the shoulder. If you have ever watched a dog doing this stretch, you will have a pretty good idea of how to do it.

There can be no knowledge of the Self to the unsteady nor can the unsteady meditate. And if there is no meditation, there is no peace. What is the possibility of peace to the unsteady, unmeditative, unpeaceful mind?

BHAGAVAD GITA, CHAPTER 2, VERSE 66, SPOKEN BY KRISHNA

1 Go onto all fours and tuck in your toes. Instead of placing your hands directly under your shoulders, let your buttocks reach back over your calves slightly and stretch your arms as far forwards as you can, while keeping the hands firmly on the ground.

2 Breathe in, and as you breathe out push up just as in the posture opposite. Push up through the arms right into the shoulder blades but be careful not to 'lock' the elbows – let them remain slightly bent to avoid unnecessary tension in the shoulders. Allow the front of the thighs to push gently backwards – this will lengthen the muscles at the back of the legs and allow the heels to release down further. Hold the posture for about six breaths and then slowly release into shankasana (see page 89) for about six breaths.

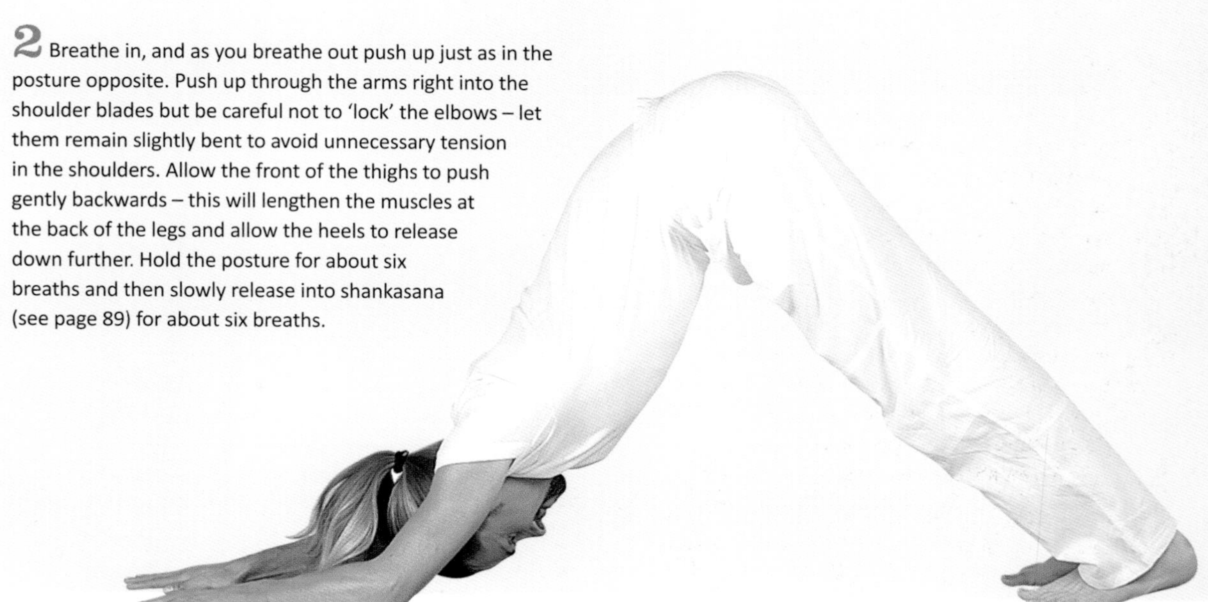

PARIVṚTTA SUPTA PĀDĀNGUṢṬHĀSANA

Rotated supine big toe posture

In this beautiful posture we learn to radiate out from our centre. In acupuncture, the point at the navel is called *Shen Que* – Gate to the Spirit Tower. About one-and-a-half inches below it is a point known as *Qi Hai* – The Sea of Qi. To the yogis, too, the pelvic basin is the receptacle of power and vitality, and it's through Manipura Chakra that this vitality can be directed to the whole body, rather than held only in the pelvic-basin area.

Borrow from the Chinese medicine imagery, and think of the entire navel area as the Pole Star of the body. If you were to stand at the North Pole and look directly upwards, it would appear as if all the stars of the heavens were rotating around one star – Polaris, situated in Ursa Minor, or the Little Dipper. This is the star ancient navigators used to make a pathway across oceans. Visualize your navel as Polaris and the rest of the body radiating out from and revolving around it when you do this posture – then the entire action of the body will flow out from this core.

To begin with, before you attempt this posture, you will need to loosen some of the very tight postural muscles of the buttocks and lower back. Use some of the stretches in the 'Warming Up' section (see pages 23–9) and also try the preliminary stretching routine shown below.

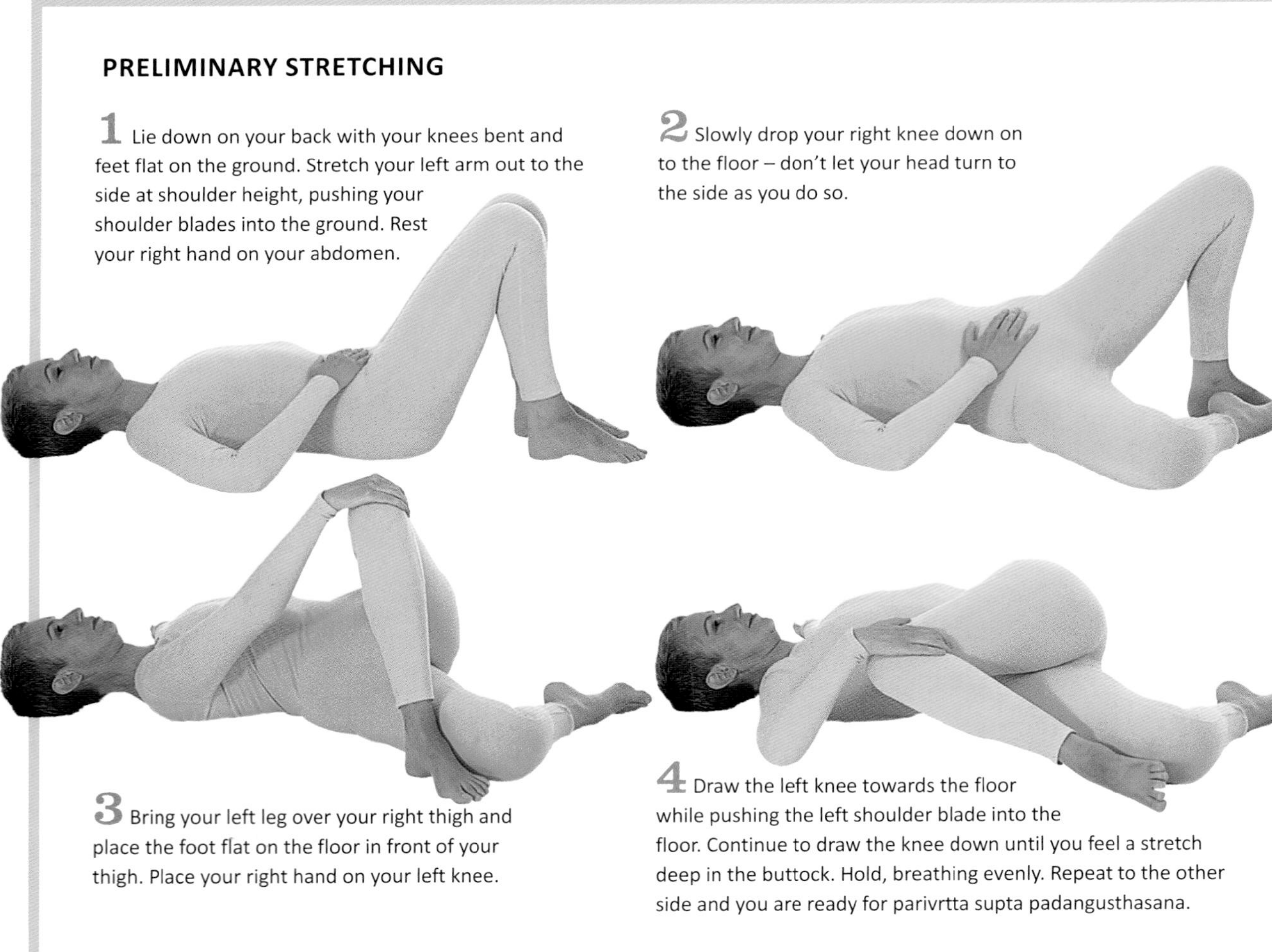

PRELIMINARY STRETCHING

1 Lie down on your back with your knees bent and feet flat on the ground. Stretch your left arm out to the side at shoulder height, pushing your shoulder blades into the ground. Rest your right hand on your abdomen.

2 Slowly drop your right knee down on to the floor – don't let your head turn to the side as you do so.

3 Bring your left leg over your right thigh and place the foot flat on the floor in front of your thigh. Place your right hand on your left knee.

4 Draw the left knee towards the floor while pushing the left shoulder blade into the floor. Continue to draw the knee down until you feel a stretch deep in the buttock. Hold, breathing evenly. Repeat to the other side and you are ready for parivrtta supta padangusthasana.

ANATOMICAL NOTES

One of the major muscles being stretched is called the piriformis (one of the lateral rotators of the leg, situated in the buttock area), and since the sciatic nerve passes either behind or through it, any tension in this muscle can be the cause of sciatica. The muscle also helps to release vitality locked into the sacroiliac joint – the most powerful weight-bearing joint of the body.

Energy steps down into physical manifestation through the bone marrow which is Ether-predominant, the joints which are Air-predominant, muscles which are Fire-predominant, tendons which are Water-predominant and bones which are Earth-predominant. Making contact at the joints is very powerful, as each of them is a nexus between Ether and Air and a source point for our physical energy.

ESOTERIC ANATOMY: THE BODY AS CONSCIOUSNESS, BRUCE BERGER

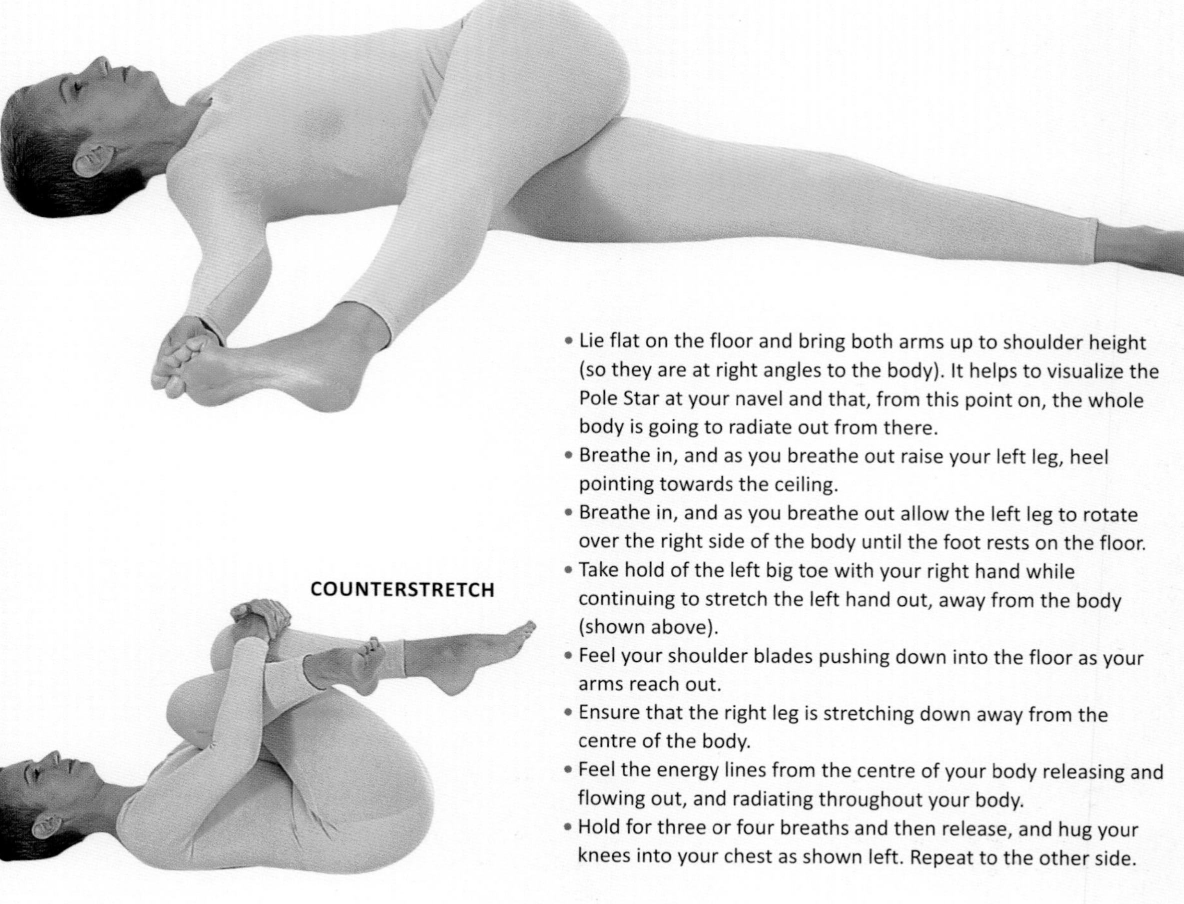

COUNTERSTRETCH

- Lie flat on the floor and bring both arms up to shoulder height (so they are at right angles to the body). It helps to visualize the Pole Star at your navel and that, from this point on, the whole body is going to radiate out from there.
- Breathe in, and as you breathe out raise your left leg, heel pointing towards the ceiling.
- Breathe in, and as you breathe out allow the left leg to rotate over the right side of the body until the foot rests on the floor.
- Take hold of the left big toe with your right hand while continuing to stretch the left hand out, away from the body (shown above).
- Feel your shoulder blades pushing down into the floor as your arms reach out.
- Ensure that the right leg is stretching down away from the centre of the body.
- Feel the energy lines from the centre of your body releasing and flowing out, and radiating throughout your body.
- Hold for three or four breaths and then release, and hug your knees into your chest as shown left. Repeat to the other side.

MATSYENDRĀSANA

Spinal twist

One of the most ancient texts of hatha yoga to have survived is the sixth-century *Hatha Yoga Pradipika* (Light of Yoga). It was written by the yogi Sri Svatmaramanath, who was a member of the esoteric nath sect, which faithfully preserved the yoga of Patanjali and the powerful practices of siddha yoga. The author names yogi Matsyendranath as the original guru of the sect who, having received it from Shiva (as Adinatha), passed it down in a lineage to Svatmarama. This beautiful posture is named after Matsyendranath, paramguru of Svatmarama. The small but deep paraspinal muscles are gently stretched and strengthened through this position.

Practice of this asana adds fuel to the digestive fire.
It becomes so bright that it burns all diseases
And awakens the serpent power
To bring equilibrium.

HATHA YOGA PRADIPIKA OF SVATMARAMA, CHAPTER 1, VERSE 27

Give your body time to warm up and get used to rotation of the spine by doing a simple twist (see below). This acts on the deepest muscles of the spine – the paraspinal, including the rotators, and the lumbar, thoracic and cervical vertebrae.

SIMPLE TWIST

1 Sit on the floor with your legs extended out in front of you. Bend your right leg and place your foot on the floor alongside your left knee. Bring your right hand over and place it on the outside of your left knee. Breathe in, and as you breathe out bring your left arm up to shoulder height and gaze at the fingertips.

2 SIDE VIEW Breathe in, and as you breathe out, slowly and gently rotate the arm around as far as you can, gazing at the fingertips all the while. Hold the posture for about five or six breaths, then return the arm to the front and release. Repeat to the other side.

1 Stretch your legs out in front of you and release your weight down through your sitting bones and legs. Let your spine flow upwards, lengthening through the front. Bend your left leg, keeping it on the floor, and place the foot alongside your right buttock. Take the right foot over the left leg and place it alongside the left thigh.

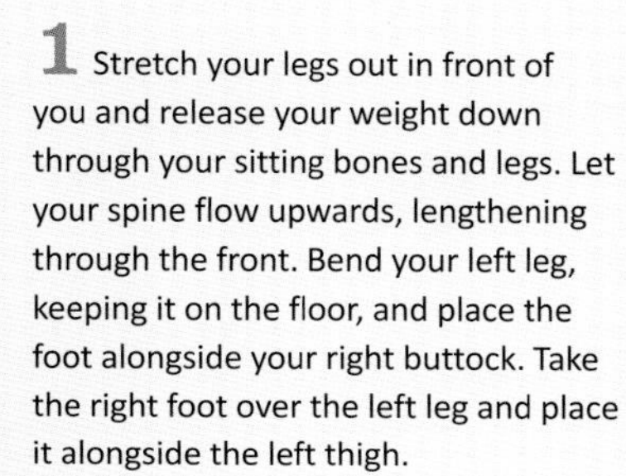

2 SIDE VIEW Twist around to the right and bring your left arm over your right knee, passing the hand under the thigh. Take your right arm back and join your hands behind you. Don't let your body collapse onto your upright thigh – rather, let the spine continue to lengthen as it rotates. Turn your head to look over your right shoulder. Hold for between five and fifteen breaths. Repeat to the other side.

VINYĀSA

Integration sequences

As we discovered earlier, postures done in sequence (such as surya namaskar) are known as a vinyasa. Once you have been doing yoga for a while you will be able to create your own vinyasas; the two sequences here will give you an idea of how to proceed. Try to choose postures from various tattvas in order to integrate these differing energies and get them working in harmony when you feel balance has been lost.

Vinyāsa I

1 Sit in vajrasana, observing your breath.
2 Come up onto your knees and swing your right leg forwards. Place your hands on the floor, still observing your breath.
3 As you breathe out, lift your arms in anjaneya asana. Feel the ribcage lifting up. Feel yourself yielding down to gravity and the hips opening and integrating. Breathe in, and as you breathe out place your hands back on the floor.
4 Breathe in, and as you breathe out swing your left leg forwards and come into uttanasana.

Vinyāsa II

1 Stand in pranamasana I, observing your breath.
2 Breathe in, and as you breathe out raise your right leg and go into natarajasana II. Hold for a few breaths.
3 Release and bend forwards slightly, letting your arms hang towards the ground.
4 Now roll down, bending your knees and allowing your spine to release, vertebrae by vertebrae, until you are resting on the balls of your feet.
5 Place your hands firmly on the floor and extend the legs, one by one, into dandasana.
6 When your posture has become steady, go into vasisthasana, supporting your weight on your left arm.
7 Return to dandasana and steady your posture.

5 Breathe in, raising your body, and go into a backbend.
6 As you breathe out, allow your head to come up and become aligned between your heels, returning to simple tadasana. Then breathe in, and as you breathe out slowly take your body forward into uttanasana once more.
7 Swing your left leg back, placing your hands on the floor, making sure that the knee and ankle align. Hold this position for a few breaths before you release.
8 Return to vajrasana and observe your breath.

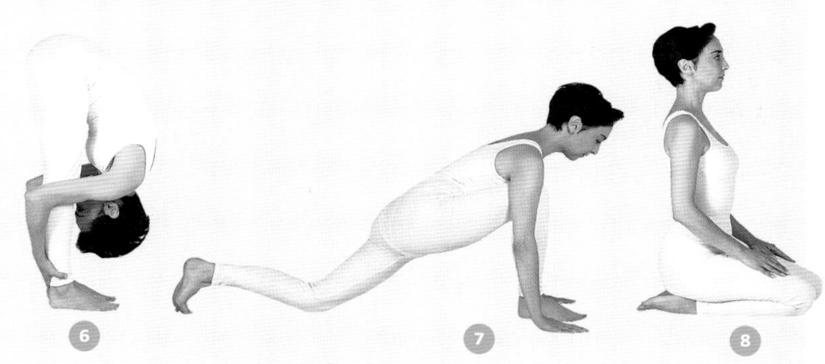

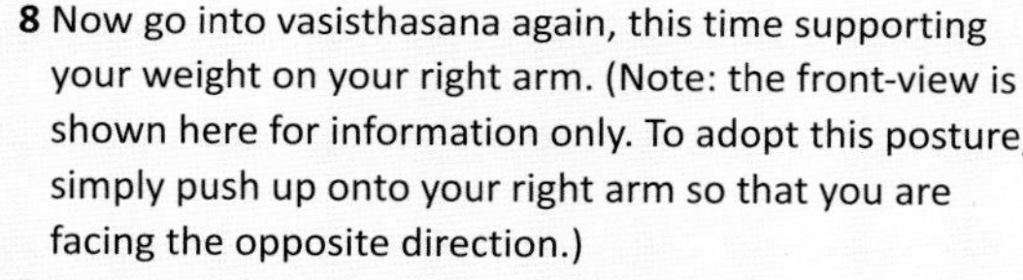

8 Now go into vasisthasana again, this time supporting your weight on your right arm. (Note: the front-view is shown here for information only. To adopt this posture, simply push up onto your right arm so that you are facing the opposite direction.)
9 Return again to dandasana and steady your posture, maintaining even breathing.
10 Gently drop down into urdhva bhujangasana on an in-breath. Don't hold this posture – immediately push back into a squatting position.
11 From this position, begin to push up slowly and gently.
12 Continue to push upwards, letting your arms and head hang towards the ground.
13 Continue pushing upwards into simple tadasana, and then raise your left leg and go into natarajasana II. Hold for a few breaths.
14 Return to pranamasana I, observing your breath.

YOGA FOR SPECIFIC AILMENTS

Hatha yoga, with its practices of asanas, pranayama, mudra and bandha, is probably the oldest known system of bodywork. Furthermore, it recognizes that consciousness is a state of the body: its nerves, its energy and its communication systems. Hatha yoga honours health as necessary for attaining the supreme goal of self-realization without tying health to physical well-being. To quote Swami Venkatesananda, 'Hatha yoga enables you to discover health which is wholeness and holiness. Health is not an absence of symptoms of sickness. Health is wholeness. It is a state of inner being in which there is no division at all.'

We can use the practice of hatha yoga to return to a balance even while we are using it as a means of self-knowledge. It is, after all, a disturbance in the tattvas – fluctuating as they do between the gunas – and a returning of them to balance that can restore a state of health in the body.

Using the tattvas, it becomes possible to devise a hatha yoga programme that addresses individual needs, and, while it's difficult to prescribe postures based entirely on symptoms, it's not impossible. We humans have been doing hatha yoga for long enough now to know which postures and breathing routines will work in a general way towards restoring wholeness and balance when confronted by various illnesses. Such postures are detailed on the following pages for a range of common ailments.

The very best assistance you can give yourself is to know yourself. As you go through this section, and perhaps work on some of the movements and asanas suggested, you will begin to understand how you can assess yourself and prescribe the best possible practices to restore yourself to health, which is 'wholeness' – and which is yoga.

BACK PAIN

Principal chakra

ALL: a loss of integration

While back pain often feels isolated to a certain area – either the lower back, the back of the neck or the lumbar region – it usually involves muscles of the whole back. Today, many of us perform almost static repetitive tasks as our jobs – for example, driving, working at a computer, standing on a shop floor or in front of a conveyor belt. The nature of these tasks is such that the muscles settle into chronic holding patterns, and our

LOWER BACK PAIN

Hamstring stretches (shortened hamstrings can be the cause of much lower back pain) pages 24 and 29

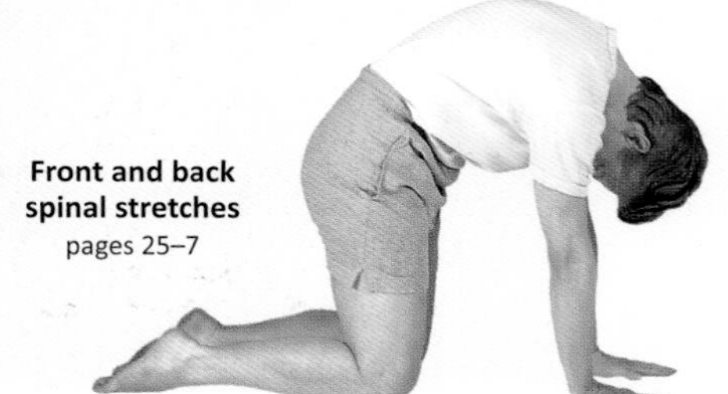

Front and back spinal stretches pages 25–7

Surya namaskar: try the first four asanas, to give the spine a good workout and stretch iliopsoas muscle, often the cause of pain). pages 117–19

Adho mukha svanasana I page 122

Matsyendrasana page 126

DEPRESSION

Principal chakra

ANAHATA

Depression is often accompanied by feelings of isolation, alienation and loneliness. Vayu Tattva, in Anahata Chakra, governs touch. The heart, called the centre of being by the yogis, needs to touch and be touched. Through touch it feels its basic connectedness with all that appears to be other. Focus your work around Anahata Chakra.

Depression can also draw us into deep introspection, from which we can emerge with a new and better understanding of ourselves. However, 'emerge' is the keyword here, so allow the whole chakra system to feel the support of the earth and do some simple movements and visualizations of Muladhara Chakra.

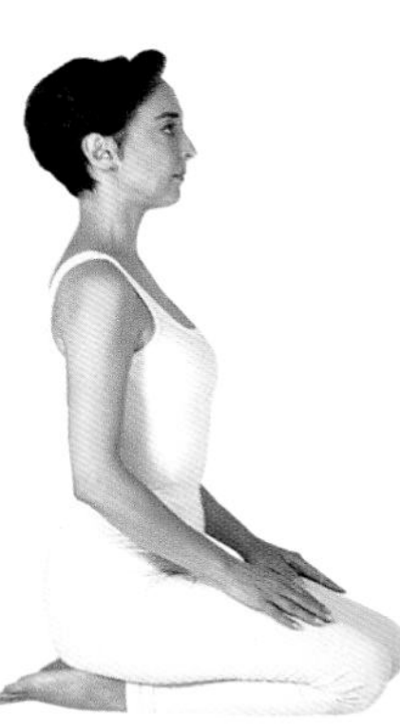

Vajrasana page 39

posture and vitality organize themselves entirely around the task we are doing. It's now possible to walk down the street and recognize the people who sit in front of computer screens all day by the forwards rotation of their shoulders, the hyperextension in the front of the neck and the pronounced thoracic curve. It's our posture, held throughout the day, that is the major cause of most back pain.

Of course, injuries play a part. If you have had a fall or a car accident – even if you didn't sustain broken bones – your muscles, disrupted from their habitual holding patterns, will respond in all kinds of ways that can be experienced as pain.

The very best thing to do is to maintain the health of the muscles of the back by ensuring that they are stretched and released regularly to restore them to their resting length.

THORACIC PAIN

Bhujangasana: do this gently, only rising as much as your back will allow. Follow with uttanasana.
page 55

Paschimottanasana
page 70

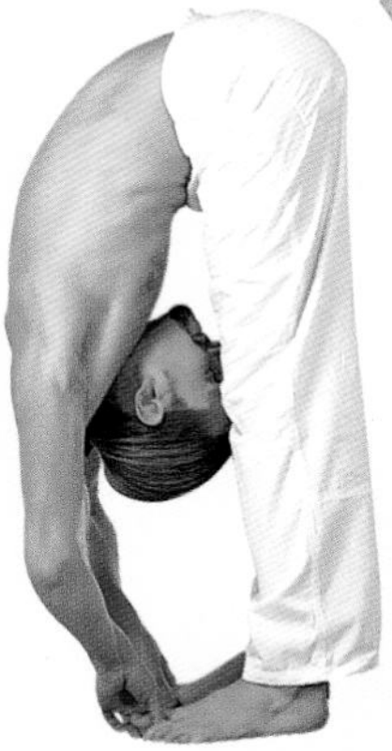

Parivrtta janusirshasana: follow with paschimottanasana
page 59

Uttanasana
page 60

Janusirshasana: follow with paschimottanasana
page 73

Ushtrasana
page 54

Bhujangasana
page 55

Adho mukha svanasana I
page 122

INSOMNIA

Principal chakra

ANAHATA

If the mind is still active when you lie down to sleep, it's almost impossible to fall asleep – no matter how tired you are. Our sympathetic nervous system is our 'get-up-and-go' call, and very often, in the stressed daily lives that we lead, it's still active when we lie down to get some rest. If you regularly suffer from insomnia, it's essential that you calm the mind and activate the parasympathetic nervous system before going to bed. Do the nadishodhana pranayama routine from the Anahata Chakra section for at least five minutes before retiring (see page 67). Once you are in bed, try the visualization from the Svadhisthana Chakra section – Apas Tattva can calm Vayu Tattva – as you are falling asleep (see page 99). Do the asanas recommended opposite before going to bed.

Ushtrasana
page 54

HIGH BLOOD PRESSURE

Principal chakra

ANAHATA and/ or **MANIPURA**

The blood circulating through the arteries and veins of our bodies is always under pressure. This pressure depends on a number of factors:

- the amount of blood in the body (a wound that causes major bleeding, for example, will cause the blood pressure to drop)
- the strength and frequency of the contractions of the heart
- the elasticity of the heart.

Generally speaking, when we are calm our blood pressure stays at a normal and constant level of around 120 over 80. The higher number is called systolic pressure, which is the blood pressure when the heart is contracted, and the lower pressure is called diastolic pressure, which is the pressure when the heart relaxes between contractions. If we become frightened or excited, this pressure reading will rise, and then return to normal once the stimulation has ceased. If, however, we have clogged or contracted arteries, the blood pressure can rise and remain at a high level. This disease is often known as the 'silent killer' because those suffering from it can be symptom-free for years. It's vital, therefore, that you get regular checks on your blood pressure and cholesterol levels (a substance we produce in the body but which, at high levels, can fur up the arteries).

Stress can be a major cause of high blood pressure, and almost all of us now lead highly stressful lives. One of the kindest things we can do for our body and our blood pressure is to get on to our yoga mats in the evening after a busy day, and do at least a twenty- or thirty-minute routine followed by some pranayama from either Svadhisthana (see page 99) or Muladhara Chakra (see page 115) before going to bed. Increasing the length of the exhalation and remaining observant during the stillpoint is an excellent way of maintaining a healthy blood-pressure level.

CAUTION

If you suffer from high blood pressure don't do any of the inverted postures or postures where your arms are raised overhead. Also, don't practise any of the bandhas.

Paschimottanasana
page 70

Anantasana
page 64

Niralambana paschimottanasana
page 86

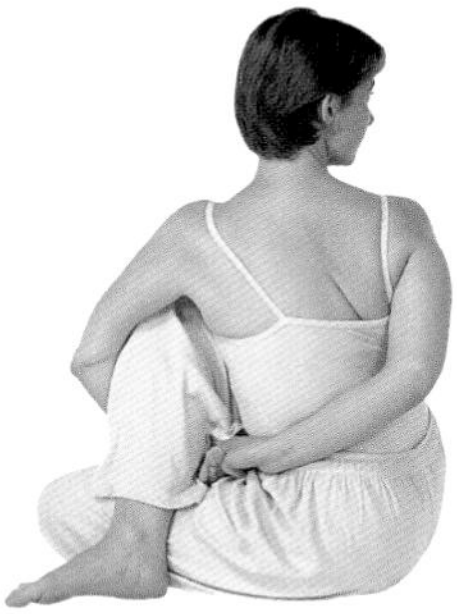

Matsyendrasana
page 126

Anjaneyasana: keep your hands in a prayer position over the heart while maintaining slow and calm breathing.
page 57

Natarajasana I: this asana is a wonderfully stabilizing posture for the whole body/vitality/mind complex; follow it with kandasana to ground your energies.
page 38

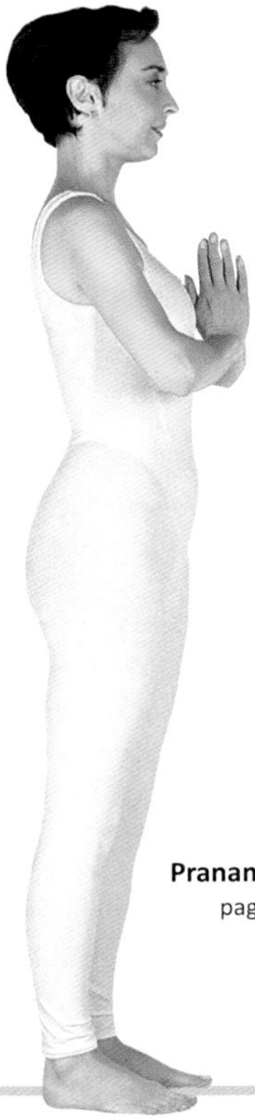

Pranamasana I
page 40

Baddha konasana
page 102

FREQUENT INFECTIONS
(COLDS AND FLU)

Principal chakra

MANIPURA

Most of us get at least one or two colds a year. Because colds are caused by viruses and we are now in such close contact with each other in urban environments – in offices, on buses and trains, in elevators – we are always in contact with those viruses. If you are constantly getting colds and flu, it may be a sign of an exhausted or lowered immune system. The chakra most closely associated with the immune system is Manipura Chakra; be sure to include some of the asanas from this chakra in your yoga practice. Also include the agnisara pranayama routine in your daily practice (see page 83) and follow it with increasing duration of the exhalations, as in Svadhisthana Chakra pranayama (see page 99).

TIRED ALL THE TIME
(TATT SYNDROME)

Principal chakra

MANIPURA

Like all other creatures on this planet, we humans absorb energy from the environment and transform it via internal cellular alchemy for our own use. This power rests with Agni Tattva contained in Manipura Chakra. Focus your attention and work on this chakra while doing some of the visualizations and pranayama for both of the chakras on either side of it.

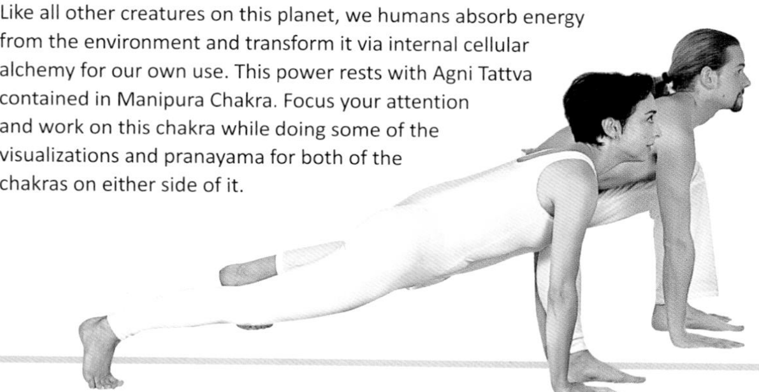

PREMENSTRUAL SYNDROME
(PMS)

Principal chakra

SVADHISTHANA

Many women report feelings of anxiety, irritability, depression, low-back pain, increased headaches, feelings of dissociation, dizziness and more in anything up to two weeks before menstruation in their monthly cycle. It's a distressing condition that can interfere with a normally vital woman who copes very well once her hormones are back in balance. One of the major factors is chronic hyperventilation (which most people are not aware they suffer from). Check your breathing: how many counts do you breathe in for, and how many do you breathe out for? We know that chronic hyperventilation causes carbon dioxide levels to drop in the blood, which can cause many of the symptoms mentioned above. Added to this, a rise in progesterone levels (which occurs in the ten days before the onset of a period) causes a further drop in carbon dioxide levels and exacerbates the whole situation. Do the breathing routines from both Svadhisthana and Muladhara Chakras to correct your breathing patterns (see pages 99 and 115), and incorporate as many of the asanas from Svadhisthana Chakra as possible in your yoga practice.

Janusirshasana
page 73

Dhanurasana
page 76

Surya namaskar
pages 117–21

Surya namaskar: try all the poses individually, and slowly move into doing them in a flowing sequence.
pages 117–21

Chakrasana
page 74

Simhasana: extend the outbreath and hold for as long as you can.
page 80

Niralambana paschimottasana
page 86

Prasarita padottanasana
page 94

Baddha konasana: occasionally incorporate this asana in your routine along with the Svadisthana Chakra asanas.
page 102

ANXIETY OR PANIC ATTACKS

Principal chakra

MULADHARA

One of the major causes of anxiety or panic attacks is hyperventilation: breathing in and out to the same value, or breathing in for longer than you breathe out. This lowers carbon dioxide levels in the blood (a condition known as hypocapnia) and the blood vessels to the brain constrict, causing less blood flow. The hyperventilation usually increases dramatically during an attack of anxiety or panic, and the person is literally left gasping for air. What they in fact need to do is to breathe in less oxygen for a while, to allow the carbon dioxide levels to rise – hence, if you are having an attack, it helps to breathe into a paper bag, so that you breathe back in some of the carbon dioxide you have exhaled. These attacks can be avoided by practising the breathing exercise shown in the Muladhara section (see page 115) on a daily basis and returning the body to a more 'normal' breathing pattern.

Parivrtta janusirshasana: to open the muscles of the ribs.
page 59

OBESITY

Principal chakra

MULADHARA

We can often find ourselves compensating for things that we lack in our lives with food. Feeling unsupported can lead us to eat carbohydrates and gain weight as we try to create support. It's often an indication of a tamasic Apas (Earth) Tattva. Add to your yoga routine as many of the postures from the Muladhara Chakra section as you can and 'stoke your internal fires' with a few asanas from Manipura Chakra. Restore harmony and balance by doing surya namaskar. The thyroid gland, situated in the throat, regulates our metabolism, and it's helpful to stimulate the gland through sarvangasana and halasana, followed by matsyasana. While doing your asanas or vinyasa (a sequence of asanas performed consecutively, without pausing), remember to keep feeling the support of the ground beneath you, and, releasing your weight into it, become aware of how lovingly the earth continues to welcome your weight and give you support.

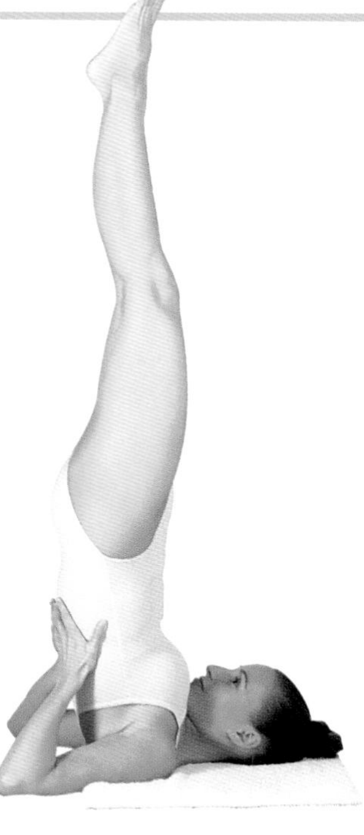

Sarvangasana
page 42

Janusirshasana
page 73

Baddha Konasana
page 102

Shankhasana: feel the movement of your lower back as you breathe.
page 89

Merudandasana
page 103

Natarajasana II
page 71

Matsyasana
page 44

Halasana
page 61

Surya namaskar
pages 117–21

ABOUT THE AUTHOR

Swami Ambikananda Saraswati is a Hindu monk who has been teaching yoga and Vedanta philosophy for more then twenty-five years. She is also an acupuncturist, massage therapist and herbalist. Her understanding of these two great Eastern systems of healing and philosophy have led to her integrating, where appropriate, their methods in her treatments. In her private clinic in Reading she combines both yoga and Chinese medicine, where appropriate, to achieve a more complete healing.

Swami Ambikananda is a disciple of the much-loved Himalayan monk, Swami Venkatesananda. She runs workshops on both the physical and philosophical aspects of yoga as well as Vedic astrology and breathwork. She teaches in the UK and abroad and is one of the founders of the Traditional Yoga Association, based in the UK, and conducts successful yoga teacher-training courses.

Through her years of study and practice, the swamini has come to see yoga as a self-discipline that must be engaged in while, paradoxically, maintaining a completely liberated intuition, in which making choices remains possible. To this end, she believes two things are of vital importance for the student: *shradda* – faith in our divine essence; and the guidance of the *sad guru*, the perfect preceptor. She is the author of *Principles of Breathwork* and *First Directions: Breathwork*. Her translations of two major Sanskrit texts, *The Uddhava Gita* and *The Katha Upanishad*, are noted for making complex philosophical concepts easy to read and understand.

THE YOGIS AND YOGINIS APPEARING IN THIS BOOK

Brahmacharini Manisha Wilmette Brown

Yogi Uddhava Samman

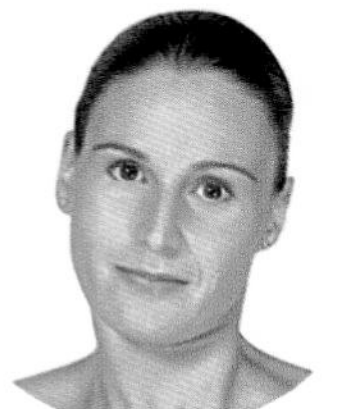

Yogini Joanne Toplass

Yogini Lorna Brazier

Yogini Samantha Newman

Yogini Karen Briscoe

Yogini Sarah Glasscock

Yogi Richard Marchant

RESOURCES

FURTHER READING

Berger, B. *Esoteric Anatomy: The Body As Consciousness*. North Atlantic Books, 1998

Bhattacharya, B. *Saivism and the Phallic World*. Munshi Ram Manohar Lal Delhi, 1993

Chaitow, L. *Modern Neuromuscular Techniques*. Churchill Livingstone, 1996

Chaitow, L. *Muscle Energy Techniques*. Churchill Livingstone, 1996

Krishnananda, S. *Yoga as a Universal Science*. The Divine Life Society, 1997

Lad, Vasant. *The Complete Book of Ayurvedic Home Remedies*. Piatkus, 1999

Smith, F. *Inner Bridges*. Humanics New Age, 1986

Sutton, K. *The Essentials of Vedic Astrology*. The Wessex Astrologer, 1999

Travell, J.G. and Simons, D.G. *Myofascial Pain and Dysfunction: The Trigger Point Manual*. William & Wilkins, 1983

Venkatesananda, S. *The Supreme Yoga*. Chiltern Yoga Trust, 1998

Venkatesananda, S. *Yoga*. Chiltern Yoga Trust, 1974

USEFUL CONTACTS

UK
The Traditional Yoga Association
www.traditionalyoga.org

Independent Yoga Network (IYN)
www.independentyoganetwork.org

USA
Yoga Alliance
www.yogaalliance.org

AUSTRALIA
Yoga Alliance Australia
www.yogaalliance.com.au

SOUTH AFRICA
Yoga Alliance South Africa
www.yogaalliance.co.za

INDEX

ACKNOWLEDGEMENTS

To all my students who over the years have inspired me to explore yoga as a means for self-discovery, and especially those who gave their time and energy to appearing in this book.

I thank John and Judy Potter for their ever-ready and helpful advice. As always, I am deeply grateful to Brahmacharini Manisha Wilmette Brown for sensitive and mindful editing.

PICTURE CREDITS

The publishers would like to thank the following sources for their kind permission to reproduce the photographs in this book: Ian Campbell 140. Steve Dunning 6.

Cover Luna Vandoorne/ShutterStockphoto.Inc

Shutterstock 2 Evgeny Atamanenko; 10 Rawpixel.com; 22 iconogenic; 32tl, 36b Fabio Lamanna; 32tr, 52b Andrekart Photography; 33tl, 68b fluke samed; 33tc, 84b Ipatov; 33tr, 100 Mykola Mazuryk

All other photography by Laura Knox

EDDISON BOOKS LIMITED

Managing Director Lisa Dyer
Creative Consultant Nick Eddison
Managing Editor Tessa Monina
Proofreader Jane Roe
Indexer Marie Lorimer
Production Sarah Rooney

This edition designed and edited by
3REDCARS
www.3redcars.co.uk
for EDDISON BOOKS LIMITED